Curiosities Series

Southwest
CURIOSITIES

Quirky characters, roadside oddities & other offbeat stuff

Sam Lowe

Guilford, Connecticut

To all the kind and gentle folks who helped locate the curiosities without hesitation or strange looks.

The prices, rates, and hours listed in this guidebook were confirmed at press time. We recommend, however, that you call establishments to obtain current information before traveling.

To buy books in quantity for corporate use or incentives, call **(800) 962-0973** or e-mail **premiums@GlobePequot.com.**

Text design: Bret Kerr

Layout artist: Casey Shain

Project editor: Lauren Szalkiewicz

Maps Alena Joy Pearce © Morris Book Publishing, LLC

All photos by the author unless otherwise noted

ISBN: 978-0-7627-5664-3

Printed in the United States of America

10 9 8 7 6 5 4 3 2 1

contents

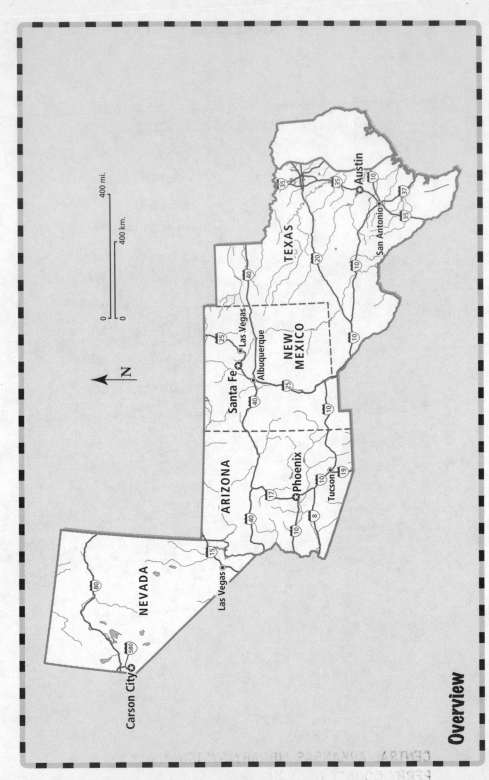

Overview

an overall introduction to uniquity

★ ★

We, those extraordinary few who seek out, expose, and glorify the unusual, are often confronted with such questions as, "Why do you want to know about that funny-looking building?" and "Who'd be interested in that old thing that's been standing in the same spot for years?"

And our answers are usually the same:

"Because it's there."

And, "You'd be surprised how many people want to know about a rock that somebody painted to look like a duck."

Which may or may not be an exaggeration. But we persist.

In our persistence, we uncover (and exploit) an outstanding variety of items that may be commonplace to those who live with them on a daily basis, but are unique to the rest of us. So we hunt them down, scribble notes about them, take photos of them, categorize them, and write about them. While we who chase and report on these unique items, places, and people are often considered strange—even weird—we continue our quest with determination and dedication for one particular reason.

It is this:

We live with the hope that you, the consumer who buys our books, will have as much fun reading about our discoveries as we did finding them.

Sam Lowe
December 2012

v

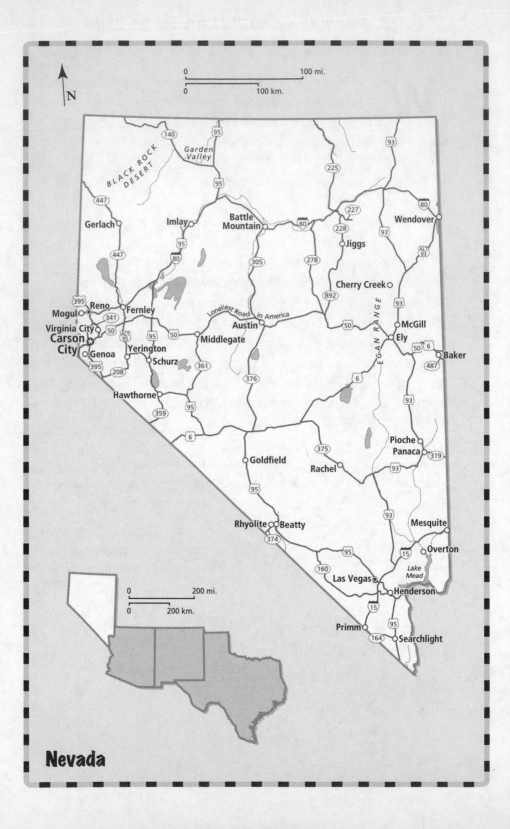

1

Nevada

According to author *Richard Moreno, who wrote* Nevada Curiosities, *Nevada is a bit like actress Maureen Stapleton in the 1978 Woody Allen movie* Interiors. *It's a place that's just a little bit louder than it ought to be, a little bit brighter than it needs to be, and, perhaps, a little bit less cultured than it wants to be. It's a curious mixture of liberal attitude—it's the only state with legal prostitution and was the first state to legalize gambling—and populist conservatism—it is the home of the "Sagebrush Rebellion," a movement to turn control of government-supervised public lands over to private hands.*

Many of those who come here intend to stay for only a short time. But then, something happens to keep them around. They learn to correctly pronounce the name (it's "Nuh-va-duh"), and also discover that even though the town of Verdi was named after the Italian composer, it's not pronounced like his name (it's not "Ver-dee," it's "Ver-dye, Nuh-va-duh"). Intrigued by those uncommonalities, they stick around and try to find out what else is weird about the state.

And there's plenty.

They discover that Nevada does things in its own curious way. For example, one of the most popular sights on a lonely highway that spans the center of the state is a giant cottonwood tree filled with hundreds of pairs of shoes. And there's a dirt road in a remote northern corner of the state lined with large boulders that have been carved with fortune

cookie–type sayings like, "The human race is like a watch; it takes all the parts to make it work."

Nevada boasts a man-made geyser, displays a sack of flour in a museum, burns a homemade statue once a year, and uses out-dated ammunition to build dirt mounds. Across the state, there is an earthen artwork that measures more than a mile long, a giant neon cowboy that waves at tourists, a 1,350-piece sterling silver dining set, and a $16,000 courthouse that cost more than $1 million.

They're all part of Nevada. A very curious Nevada.

Mr. Stokes's Summer Cottage
Austin

Anson Phelps Stokes was so rich that in 1896, when he decided to build a summer house for his two sons so they could keep an eye on his mining and railroad properties in Austin, he opted for something grand and unusual—he wanted a stone castle that resembled a villa he had seen outside Rome.

The original McMansion: Stokes Castle is a strange house built by a rich guy who hardly lived in it.
RICHARD MORENO

The seasonal home, known today as Stokes Castle, was unlike any-thing else in Austin. Erected on the west side of the Toiyabe Range, about a mile from Austin, it rose three stories high and was built of slabs of native granite held in position by wedging and clay mortar. Wooden balconies surrounded the second and third stories, and each floor had a fireplace. The first floor contained the kitchen and dining room (the place had indoor plumbing), while the second level served as a living room. The top floor had two bedrooms and the roof was a battlemented terrace with an open-air viewing area that looked out on the Reese River Valley.

After the structure was completed in 1897, the family lived in it for about a month that summer, then left and never returned. It wasn't a money problem, however. Stokes was a member of one of America's wealthiest families. He had made his fortune in banking before becoming involved in mining in Nevada. In the 1870s, he financed construction of the Nevada Central Railroad, which ran from Austin to Battle Mountain. Later, he built a grand estate called Shadowbrook in Massachusetts, which at that time was the largest private residence in the nation.

Once abandoned, the castle fell into disrepair. The balconies, interior floors, and roof all collapsed, and local kids climbed inside and scratched their names into the walls. A few decades ago, a fence was erected around the landmark, now privately owned, and a stone marker was installed adjacent to the tower to explain its history. A narrow dirt road about a half-mile west of Austin leads to the site off US Highway 50.

The World's Most Profitable Sack of Flour
Austin

April 19, 1864, was Election Day in Austin. For the occasion, two prominent local businessmen, store owner Reuel Gridley and Doctor Herrick, agreed to a wager that should the mayoral candidate sup-ported by either man win, the other would carry a fifty-pound sack of flour along the town's main street while whistling a political tune.

Herrick's candidate won, so a few weeks after the election, the shop-
keeper hoisted a sack of flour on his shoulder and began his walk
while whistling "Old John Brown." A parade of local officials, the
town band, and several horseback riders formed a procession and led
Gridley through the community. When the one-mile trek ended, politicians gave speeches, and Gridley auctioned off the sack of flour, with
proceeds going to the Sanitary Fund, the Civil War predecessor to the
Red Cross.

But after the sale was completed, the buyer returned the sack to
Gridley and urged him to auction it off again. This ritual continued
throughout the day, and by the end of the action, more than four
thousand dollars had been raised for charity.

Other communities heard about Gridley's famous sack of flour, and
he was invited to conduct similar auctions throughout Nevada and
the West. During the next year, Gridley traveled all over the West and
raised an estimated $275,000 for the aid fund. But his success came
at a cost. Due to the frequent absences, his business took a downturn
and he was forced to close it. The store is still standing and has been
converted into a local museum.

The sack of flour is still around, too. In the early twentieth century,
Gridley's family donated it to the Nevada Historical Society in Reno,
which has it on display in its facility at 1650 North Virginia Street.
It's open Wednesday through Saturday. For more information, call
(775) 688-1190 or go to museums.nevadaculture.org and select the
"Historical Society, Reno" link.

The Permanent Wave Society
Baker

When the muse hits Nevadans, they are capable of turning nearly
anything into a thing of beauty (keeping in mind that beauty is quite
subjective). That explains the displays of unusual public art along
Route 488, the road leading from the tiny settlement of Baker to the
entrance of Great Basin National Park. There, seemingly spontaneous

★ ★

outbursts of artistic expression can be found along the posts lining the road.

Apparently, the impetus for this creativity was the late Doc Sherman, a Baker resident and artist who, in a bit of whimsy in the mid-1990s, attached rubber gloves filled with cement to the top of a fence post and named it *The Permanent Wave*. This gave birth to the Permanent Wave Society, a sort of loose-knit coalition of friends and neighbors who have added more pieces of artwork. Over the years, several dozen more art objects have been placed on or near the fence.

Many, like the rusting hulk of an old car driven by the skeleton of a horse and known as *Horse With No Name*, are definitely eye-catching. Others rely on visual humor or puns, such as the head of a space crea-ture holding a ski, a large rubber dinosaur wearing a bib and holding a fork, and a wooden face that has CDs for its eyes, nose, and mouth and is wearing an eye patch.

Doc Sherman, who began creating his work as therapy after being partially paralyzed by a stroke, passed away in 2004. But other artists keep the spirit of the society alive by freshening up his work and add-ing new ones.

Flat and Boring Can Be Good
Battle Mountain

It's not often that something ordinary and mundane can thrust a place into prominence. But that's what happened to north-central Nevada's Battle Mountain when it was discovered that the community is the site of a four-mile stretch of frontage road so straight and flat that it is the ideal place to race human-powered vehicles.

In the 1990s, the World Human-Powered Vehicle Association deter-mined that Route 305, just outside Battle Mountain, is "one of the straightest, flattest and smoothest surfaces in the world." In 1999, the group, which oversees the setting of speed records made by member vehicles, began hosting the World Human-Powered Speed Challenge here.

✱ ✱

Since then, dozens of riders, most racing customized recumbents (bicycle-like devices ridden in the seated or supine position) made of high-tech, lightweight materials, have flocked to Battle Mountain and attempted to break world records for pedal-powered units. In the rarefied high desert air, multiple records have been set and shattered over the years. Riders have an acceleration zone of about four miles to reach their maximum velocity before being timed crossing the official two-hundred-meter distance. Some of the times are admirable. For example, in 2002 American racer Sam Whittington set a solo rider sprint record of eighty-one miles per hour.

For more information, plug World Human-Powered Vehicle Association into any search engine and it'll reveal reams of background and statistics.

The Story of Melvin and Howard
Beatty

Melvin Dummar still insists that he met Howard Hughes on a cold December night in 1967. He says he was driving on US Highway 95 from his home in Gabbs, Nevada, to Los Angeles when he pulled over to take a leak. While relieving himself, he spotted a frail, bearded old man lying on the side of the lonely, two-lane dirt road. He checked and found the man was alive, but a little delirious. So he helped him into his car and agreed to take him to Las Vegas.

Warmed by the car heater, the old man listened as Dummar talked about how he had once tried to get a job at Hughes Aircraft Company. The man perked up and said he could help because he was Howard Hughes and he owned the company. Dummar said he was amused, but figured the man had been out in the desert too long. Once in Las Vegas, his passenger directed Dummar to drop him off at the Sands Hotel, where Hughes lived during the late 1960s.

After the reclusive billionaire died a few years later, a will mysteriously surfaced in Salt Lake City that named Dummar as a one-sixteenth beneficiary of the Hughes fortune. However, because the

★ ★

It was on a lonely stretch of US 95 near Beatty—like this one—that Melvin Dummar stumbled on Howard Hughes.

RICHARD MORENO

will had never been formally filed, its authenticity was immediately questioned. Following legal challenges, the will was ruled a fake, and many claimed that Dummar concocted the whole scheme. In 1980, an Academy Award–winning movie, *Melvin and Howard*, was filmed, based on the claim. Dummar spent much of the money he received from the movie rights defending his story in court.

In 2005, Dummar was once again thrust into the public spotlight after the publication of a book written by a former FBI agent seemed to verify his story. The agent, Gary Magnesen, wrote that records and witnesses indicated that Hughes was in remote central Nevada at that time. A former Hughes pilot claimed to have flown the industrialist to a brothel about six miles north of where he was picked up by Dummar. As a result, Dummar filed a lawsuit in 2006 and again asked for his share of the will, an estimated $156 million. A year later, however, a Utah judge tossed out the suit.

But Dummar, now living in northern Utah, still maintains that he really did meet Howard Hughes in the desert on that December night.

Burning Man
Black Rock Desert

Based on the media attention given to the annual Burning Man celebration, you might think the event is some kind of pagan-hippie-anarchist-druggie-nudist-apocalyptic-love-in freakfest. Typical images show half-naked, brightly painted, flamboyantly costumed men and women frolicking on the dusty flats of Black Rock Desert in September. The coverage usually includes scenes of the traditional igniting of the Burning Man, a giant wooden figure that is the symbol of the festival.

But those who attend and organize the event insist that's not an accurate picture. Although plenty of people are naked, half-naked, painted, or wearing outrageous attire, and there is the burning of the giant man, the event is really "an endless spectacle of self-expression," according to founder Larry Harvey, who also called it "a carefully crafted social experiment."

Of course, what Burning Man is depends on the participant. It now attracts up to fifty thousand people every year, including stockbrokers from San Francisco, organic farmers from Corvallis, and video game programmers from Provo. They all shed the trappings of their regular lives and, for a week, become a part of the bold experiment. The result is a sort of organized chaos in the desert. But there are rules. One of the primary ones is to bring only what you need to survive in the desert, and take everything you bring back out.

The event started in 1986 when Harvey and friend Jerry James built an eight-foot-tall wooden man figure on San Francisco's Baker Beach to honor the summer solstice, then burned it in front of about twenty friends. They repeated that performance every year until 1990, when they moved it to the Black Rock Desert due to increasing tensions between the burners and the San Francisco police.

Attendance has grown every year since, and the celebration has expanded from the simple burning of a wooden figure to a full-scale arts festival that includes a fashion show, an on-site newspaper, and a massive temporary settlement complete with themed camps and villages. Throughout the year, burners and campers keep in touch via an interactive website, burningman.com.

Jailhouse Blues
Cherry Creek

Somebody in the old mining town of Cherry Creek had a macabre sense of humor. On a hill south of the near-ghost town are the local cemeteries. Segregated by religious and ethnic identity, each contains both worn wooden markers and elegant marble tombstones and monuments. Adjacent to these fields of everlasting dreams is a decrepit, single-story log cabin. On a small sign affixed above the front door is the word JAIL. The unlikely coincidence of having a jail so close to the cemeteries is certainly enough to make one think twice about a life of crime.

The community's story is best told in a small local museum that once served as the Cherry Creek Schoolhouse. Open during the summer and only by appointment, the museum has an assortment of antiques, old bicycles, mining tools, and furniture collected from the area. The town, located about fifty miles north of Ely, has a rich history that began with the discovery of gold and silver around 1872. Within a short time, more than a thousand miners and others had flocked to the new, hot mining camp of the moment. For the next several decades, the mines of Cherry Creek (named for the chokecherry bushes that grow in the area) experienced the usual cyclical booms and busts so common to the industry.

These days, Cherry Creek boasts more ghosts than people.
PHOTO COURTESY OF THE NEVADA COMMISSION ON TOURISM

But by the mid-twentieth century, the town had settled into a state of inactivity. Today, visitors will find a handful of large relics scattered around the old town site, including a large red freight barn and the remains of several stone buildings.

The Big Stone Hives
Egan Range

Out on the edge of the Egan Range, about twelve miles south of Ely, are half a dozen thirty-foot-high rock domes that are twenty-seven feet around at the base. Although they might appear to have been made by giant bees, they're actually stone charcoal ovens erected in 1876.

★ ★

The Ward Charcoal Ovens are a hot historical attraction.
PHOTO COURTESY OF THE NEVADA COMMISSION ON TOURISM

Known as the Ward Charcoal Ovens, they once converted wood into hotter-burning charcoal, which was used to fire local mining smelters. Each kiln was layered with about thirty-five cords of wood, usually piñon pine or juniper, which were partially burned to produce the charcoal. The wood was trimmed into six-foot lengths and stacked vertically inside the domes, with access through the floor opening. Additional wood was loaded into the oven from an upper opening.

The wood was ignited, and metal doors were sealed shut. Small vents were opened and closed to control heat and air intakes. According to historians, it took eleven days to slow-burn the wood into charcoal, which was then used to smelt the gold and silver discovered in the foothills of Ward Mountain in 1872. Within three years, a mining community named Ward had sprung up with more than a thousand residents. But three years later, the mines started shutting down and the population dwindled. By the early 1900s, Ward was a ghost town and the ovens were abandoned.

But as they aged, the ovens were put to new uses as stables and emergency lodging for wandering sheepherders and cowboys. According to local legend, the interior of one was painted white and a bed was hauled inside so it could serve as a honeymoon suite for a gambler and his fiancée. But the wedding was called off. Apparently, the bride didn't want to spend such an important night in a drafty old charcoal oven.

In the 1950s, the ovens were acquired by the Nevada Division of State Parks, which added picnic tables, hiking trails into the Egan Range, and a few campsites. The site is open daily from sunrise to sunset. For more information, visit the website parks.nv.gov/parks/ward-charcoal-ovens-state-historic-park.

Painting the Town Red (and Other Colors)
Ely

Murals on buildings aren't anything particularly new, but the town of Ely has taken wall-size paintings to a new level. In the last few years, more than twenty building walls in the former copper-mining center have been transformed from blank brick or concrete surfaces to works of art.

Ely's mural project began in 1999, when local businessman Norm Goeringer hired Nevada cowboy artist Larry Bute to paint a giant mural titled *Cattle Drive* on the side of his building on the corner of Aultman and Fourth streets. The work depicts a Nevada Northern Railway locomotive and a cattle drive.

Other businesses took note, and several commissioned Bute to paint western murals on their buildings. Eventually, the Ely Renaissance Society, a nonprofit group, formed and began raising money to

★ ★

**What do you call a colorful painting on the wall of
an old building? Art, of course.**
PHOTO COURTESY OF THE NEVADA COMMISSION ON TOURISM

transform empty walls into huge murals. Ely has experienced economic
turmoil as its once-thriving copper-mining industry faded in the 1980s.
The murals have become a way to help Ely attract attention and tourists. In 2004, the large paintings helped the town host the Global
Mural Conference, which brought about a hundred mural artists and
other culture experts to town for several days.

Most of the murals have western themes that reflect historical
events or scenes representative of the area's past. Bute has painted
several of them; others have also contributed and now, a walking tour
of the murals is like leafing through a photo album of the community's
roots.

★ ★

The Loneliest Road(s) in America?

Fernley

If you want to be alone, really alone, this is a good place to start. In 1986, *Life* magazine described the 287-mile stretch of US Highway 50 between Fernley and Ely as the "Loneliest Road in America." The magazine said the chunk of pavement had few points of interest, and urged travelers to have "survival skills" to make the journey. In response, the communities along the route—Ely, Eureka, Austin, Fallon, and Fernley—worked with the Nevada Commission on Tourism to develop a tongue-in-cheek "Highway 50 Survival Kit" containing brochures and maps detailing places along the highway.

Additionally, a road game was created that urged those who drove the road to stop in each of the communities and have a Highway 50 map stamped by a local business or chamber of commerce. The validated maps could be redeemed for an official "Loneliest Road Survivor" certificate and other souvenirs. In 1988, the Nevada Legislature officially declared US Highway 50 across Nevada as the "Loneliest Road in America" and had signs bearing that designation posted across the route.

But is it really all *that* lonely?

Not according to the Nevada Transportation Department, which reports that an average of about 650 vehicles per day hit the pavement at its loneliest point, near Austin. In fact, US Highway 50 is not even the loneliest road in Nevada. For example, Route 121 from US Highway 50 to the Dixie Valley gets a mere ten cars per day in both directions. Route 722 from Eastgate to Austin—the original path of US Highway 50 in the center of the state—sees a total of only forty-five vehicles per day.

But US Highway 50 definitely is one of the state's most historic routes. In 1859, Captain James H. Simpson led a US Army Topographical Corps mapping expedition along the route. His findings helped the founders of the Pony Express select that trail when they established their legendary mail service about a year later. Although

Bring your own company if you're crossing the "Loneliest Road in America." RICHARD MORENO

the Pony Express stayed in business only for about eighteen months, the road (as well as many of the Pony Express stations) was soon incorporated into the Overland Stagecoach and Mail line. Early in the twentieth century, the central Nevada route was chosen to be part of the first transcontinental automobile road, the Lincoln Highway. In the 1920s, the Lincoln Highway was absorbed into the federal highway system and became US Highway 50.

It's easy to become a proud survivor of a journey on "the Loneliest Road." Each month, the Nevada Tourist department continues to mail out hundreds of Survival Kits, which were spruced up in 2006 for the twentieth anniversary of the *Life* story. To download or view this guide, go to travelnevada.com/guides-brochures and scroll down to the "Nevada Highway 50 Survival Guide."

Nevada's Not-So-Natural Geyser
Fly Geyser

Fly Geyser is a spectacular sight as it spews clouds of hot water about four or five feet high in the air. The geyser consists of three large, travertine mounds that rise out of a field of tall reeds and grasses, with a series of terraces around the base. In addition to the spraying hot

One of Nevada's oddest "natural" wonders is the man-made Fly Geyser on the edge of the Black Rock Desert.
RICHARD MORENO

uncapped or was improperly plugged. As a result, the scalding water was allowed to blast uncontrolled from the hole, and calcium carbonate deposits began to form, growing several inches each year.

Now, after a few decades, those deposits have become large mounds taller than the average man. Scientists say the green and reddish coloring on the outside of the mounds is the result of thermophilic algae, which flourish in moist, hot environments.

Interestingly, the circumstances that created Fly Geyser apparently occurred at least once before. Around 1917, a well was drilled a few hundred feet north of the geyser. That well was also abandoned, and over time a massive ten- to twelve-foot-high calcium carbonate cone formed. Today, no hot water flows from the older mound; apparently it dried up when water was naturally diverted to the newer one.

The geyser is about twenty miles north of Gerlach via Route 34, but it's on private property so don't trespass. But the water plumes are easily visible from the road.

And Now, Some Really, Really Big Art
Garden Valley

Artist Michael Heizer doesn't talk much about his work. In the past thirty years, he has agreed to only two interviews, both with the *New York Times*. However, his magnum opus, which he's been working on since 1971, speaks volumes. Called *City*, the project is earthen art of unprecedented size—it covers a space about one and a quarter miles long and more than a quarter-mile wide.

Heizer is an environmental artist who specializes in creating works in the natural world. For *City*, he is using concrete, rock, and massive mounds of dirt to craft a work designed to rival the Native American mounds of the Midwest and the ancient cities of Central and South America. He says he came up with the idea after spending time in the Yucatan studying Chichen Itza. He was already at the forefront of the art movement that became known as Land Art, Earth Art, or Environmental Art. In 1969, he completed *Double Negative*, a fifteen-hundred-foot-long, fifty-foot-deep, thirty-foot-wide slice gouged out of a mesa near Overton, Nevada.

His work *City* is a series of complexes, with each containing mounds and structures spread over hundreds of acres and some reaching heights up to eighty feet. On his fan website, Heizer says, "As long as you're going to make a sculpture, why not make one that competes with a 747, or the Empire State building, or the Golden Gate Bridge."

Limited financial resources slowed his project in the 1980s, but two private art foundations have agreed to fund the completion. Although originally scheduled to be done by 2010, it's still a work in progress, so it's not yet open to the public. Because, as the artist told a reporter, "All these rubberneckers show up as if it's entertainment. People fly over the place. This is private property. People presume that I want them to see it. That is a rash presumption. . . . The work isn't cohesive yet. When I finish Phase 5, O.K."

The Confectionery Ball

Genoa

In 1919, the tiny community of Genoa wanted to purchase street-lights. Because they didn't have a tax base, the citizens decided to hold a "Candy Dance" to raise money for the public illumination. Lillian Virgin Finnegan, daughter of a local judge, suggested the dance as well as the idea of passing candy around during the affair. She believed that the free, homemade sweets would attract a better turn-out for the event, which would also include a midnight dinner at the Raycraft Hotel.

Finnegan and her aunt, Jane Raycraft Campbell, persuaded most of the women in Genoa to cook up the confections, and the dance was a big success, raising enough money to purchase the streetlights. But the townspeople quickly realized that they also needed money to pay for the electricity required to keep them operating. So they decided to hold the Candy Dance every year, with the proceeds paying for a year's worth of electricity.

Since then, the dance and dinner have become an annual affair.
And although the town has only 250 residents, each year they sell
four thousand pounds of homemade fudge, divinity, and other tasty
sweets, along with other food and T-shirts. In recent years, the dance

**The Genoa Candy Dance includes an arts and crafts fair
and a candy sale to raise money for the town's services.**
RICHARD MORENO

has generated ninety thousand to one hundred thousand dollars annually, with the proceeds going toward community projects.

In the 1970s, an arts and crafts fair was added to boost attendance. A dozen vendors showed up the first year; now the fair is held over two days and has about 350 exhibitor booths spread over the Mormon Station Historic State Monument and the Genoa Town Park, and attendance has spurted to more than eighty thousand people.

Snowshoe Thompson

Genoa

One of the nearly forgotten figures in Nevada history is Jon Torsteinson Rui, better known as John "Snowshoe" Thompson. He is credited

Grave of John "Snowshoe" Thompson, the man you can blame for snowboarders
RICHARD MORENO

with introducing skiing to northern California and Nevada. Prior to his arrival in the region in the mid-1850s, no one had ever strapped on a pair of thin, wooden boards and slid down a hill.

Thompson was born in Norway in 1827. When he was ten years old, his family immigrated to America and settled in the Midwest. In 1851, however, John joined the thousands of people heading to California to mine for gold. Eventually, he was hired to carry mail between Placerville, California, and Genoa, Nevada. In order to make the trek in the winter, he crafted a pair of wooden skis. For the next two decades, Thompson delivered the mail in small towns throughout the Sierra Nevada.

Word spread about Thompson's "Norwegian snowshoes." He taught dozens of people how to glide across the snow and almost single-handedly introduced skiing to the region. Thompson died in 1876 and is buried in the quiet Genoa cemetery, which is located fifteen miles southwest of Carson City via US Highway 395 and Jack's Valley Road. The gravesite is at the rear of the cemetery, under large shade trees. Today, visitors can pay their respects to the father of Sierra Nevada skiing and view his unique tombstone, featuring a pair of skis carved into the white marble.

Set in Stone
Gerlach

DeWayne "Doobie" Williams was one of a kind. Williams, who died in 1995, spent the last two decades or so of his life carving clever, pithy, and even bizarre comments onto large boulders lining a dirt road on the edge of Black Rock Desert about four miles north of Gerlach, just off Route 34 (there's a sign on the left marked GURU ROAD.) Williams also crafted weird art pieces from animal bones, scraps of wood, and assorted trash to visually enhance some of his sayings. He named the site of his creations Guru Road or Dooby Avenue.

Williams was born near Gerlach and earned his nickname because apparently he did inhale. His efforts began when he started chiseling

On Doobie's road are many quips and phrases that make you think about the issues he raises.
PHOTO COURTESY OF THE NEVADA COMMISSION ON TOURISM.

his name onto a rock. Pleased with the result, he added stones with the names of friends and local residents. Soon, Williams was placing the carved stones along a Bureau of Land Management road on the eastern side of the Granite Mountains a few miles north of Gerlach. He also began to expand the messages, writing brief, thought-provoking passages on the rocks. One said, "The human race is like a watch, it takes all the parts to make it work." Another declared, "To crush the simple atom all mankind was intent, and now the atom will return the compliment."

As time went by, he grew more whimsical and erected elaborate folk art creations, such as a stump-and-bone tree and a tribute to Elvis Presley. He built a small structure that has old television screens for

★ ★

windows and named it the *Desert Broadcasting System*. Other exhibits addressed weightier issues such as nuclear weapons and the Vietnam War. And because he had served in Japan shortly after the atomic bombs were dropped, he created *Ground Zero*, a depiction of an A-bomb blast made of different colored rocks.

In 2005, a rock slide covered a large portion of Guru Road, but much of the site has been restored with the help of the Friends of Black Rock/High Rock and other volunteers, who conduct a Guru Road Restoration effort each June.

No Spitting Allowed
Goldfield

There's a sign in the hallway outside the courtroom in the Esmeralda County Courthouse stating GENTLEMEN WILL NOT EXPECTORATE IN THE HALLWAY. Inside, the courtroom, which originally cost $125,000, boasts original Tiffany stained-glass lamps and high-end frontier accents, like brass gaslight fixtures and wire loops underneath the wooden courtroom seats where a visitor can safely stow his or her cowboy hat. It's a classy hall of justice.

Built in 1907–08, the imposing stone courthouse hints at Goldfield's past grandeur. Gold was discovered there in 1902, and within a few years the community had ballooned into Nevada's largest city with about twenty thousand residents. The ore, however, was about a mile wide but only an inch deep. So, after about a decade of prosperity, Goldfield's boom was over, and the population quickly dwindled.

But unlike many Nevada mining towns, Goldfield never completely faded away. The courthouse, which has remained in operation throughout the years, is one of the best-maintained buildings in town. The mission-revival structure has a dramatic, castle-like appearance created by its coarse stone exterior; a tall, stepped parapet at the roofline above the entrance; and notched walls at the four corners.

Inside are finely crafted wood staircases, ornate light fixtures, and expensive furnishings, including the Tiffany lamps. But if you want to

The elegant Esmeralda County Courthouse in Goldfield boasts Tiffany lamps, brass fixtures, and a "no spitting" sign.
PHOTO COURTESY OF THE NEVADA COMMISSION ON TOURISM

see the lamps, you'll have to ask a court employee to unlock the doors because, a few years ago, a visitor was caught trying to remove them from the judge's bench.

Goldfield is about 185 miles north of Las Vegas. The courthouse is located at 233 Crook Street (US Highway 95).

Those Exploding Mounds
Hawthorne

From the air, the town of Hawthorne looks as though giant earthen and grass-covered caterpillars surround it. More than 2,400 dirt and concrete humps spread out across the flat valley around this community of about 3,700 residents. The brown, oblong bunkers are filled with an estimated 300,000 tons of military ammunition, about half of which is so old that it is scheduled for disposal.

The mounds, which cover some 147,000 acres, were built with steel-reinforced concrete blast walls designed to explode upward if there are accidental detonations like those that occurred in 1984 and again in the early 1990s.

Surprisingly, most Hawthornians are pretty laid back about the town's status as the place most likely to be blasted off the face of the earth. In fact, they embrace their heritage as the nation's bomb stockpile—one of the town's main attractions is the Hawthorne Ordnance Museum, which celebrates the area's four-decade history as a weapons storehouse. Located inside a former car dealership, the museum displays a variety of now-harmless weapons of mass destruction, including torpedoes, land mines, bombs, guns, and other former instruments of war.

Hawthorne became America's munitions dump after a devastating explosion at the Naval Ammunition Depot at Lake Denmark, New Jersey, in 1927. The blast demolished the depot and adjacent arsenal, and severely damaged surrounding communities. Twenty-one people died, and another fifty-three were seriously injured. The federal government immediately began looking for a more remote, less populated place for use as an ammo storehouse. Hawthorne, then a town of about five hundred, was selected and, at first, the storehouse was a major asset to the community. The military employed more than 5,600 people at the depot, which became the weaponry staging area for the nation's World War II effort. By 1944, Hawthorne had a population of thirteen thousand.

But it's been a downhill slide ever since. After the war, the government cut back on the number of employees and eventually outsourced the plant to a private firm. In 2005, a federal military base-closure commission recommended shutting down the depot, which would have meant the loss of half the town's jobs. But Nevada's congressional delegation successfully fought to keep it open.

The Ordnance Museum, located on the corner of Ninth and E Streets, is open Monday through Friday from 10 a.m. to 4 p.m., and on Saturday from 10 a.m. to 2 p.m. Admission is free. For more information, call (775) 945-5400.

Nevada's Willy Wonka

Henderson

The best part of a visit to the Ethel M Chocolate Factory in Henderson is the end. That's when you're ushered into the lounge and provided with a free sample. Of course, that's not to say the rest of the tour isn't worthwhile. For one thing, it's free. And it's interesting.

The Ethel M Chocolate Factory's garden of succulents
PHOTO COURTESY OF THE LAS VEGAS NEWS BUREAU

The story of Ethel M Chocolates began in 1976, when retired seventy-two-year-old candy king Forrest Mars Sr. (creator of M&Ms, Milky Way, Snickers, and other candies) decided to jump back into the confectionery business with a gourmet chocolate label. He specialized in liqueur-filled chocolates, which were originally sold only in Nevada.

The company grew and evolved. After Mars died in 1999, the product line was expanded beyond rum- and Kahlua-filled chocolates to a variety of gourmet treats. In 2005, the company began rebranding its Ethel M retail outlets, which had grown to nineteen in Nevada and Illinois, into Ethel's Chocolate Lounge, an upscale, sit-down dessert cafe that sells chocolate fondue, truffles, tea, hot cocoa, and a variety of chocolate-flavored beverages and candies.

But the factory remains the heart and soul of the company. And the Ethel M name lives on in the classic collection, which includes Almond Butter Krisps, Lemon Satin Cremes, Milk Chocolate Raspberry Satin Cremes, and the Ethel M Buttery Pecan Brittle. Visitors can take a self-guided tour that passes by the main candy-making rooms, visible behind glass walls. An overhead video presentation explains that the company uses a special formula to make its gourmet chocolate while thousands of little round candies march by on a conveyor belt.

The factory is also home to a giant botanical garden filled with hundreds of species of desert plants, primarily cactus. It spreads across two and a half acres, and a series of concrete pathways winds past interpretive signs that explain each species.

The factory and garden are located about seven miles southeast of the Las Vegas Strip at 2 Cactus Garden Drive in Henderson.

Nevada's State Bush

Nevada's state flower is a scruffy shrub. Unlike many states, which have beautiful flowers like roses or camellias as their official floral species, Nevada's flower is sagebrush, a fragrant, green-gray plant formally known as *Artemisia tridentata*. Technically, it is a member of the wormwood family. It can grow up to twelve feet high, seems to survive in the most inhospitable of places, and serves as an important winter food for cattle and sheep.

Although sagebrush is found nearly everywhere in the state, it is not exactly beloved. Onetime Nevadan Mark Twain described it as the "fag-end of vegetable creation" and wrote that "when crushed, sagebrush emits an odor which isn't exactly magnolia and equally isn't polecat—but is sort of a compromise between the two." He also called it only a "fair" fuel and claimed that nothing could abide its flavor save "the jackass and his illegitimate child, the mule."

Comedian Johnny Carson was once so amused by the fact that Nevada's state flower was a bush that he held up a scraggly cluster of sagebrush branches and asked his audience to imagine sending a bouquet to a wife or girlfriend for Valentine's Day.

On the other hand, author Robert Laxalt, who spent nearly his entire life in Nevada, felt far more kindly toward the shrub. He wrote of being abroad when he received a letter from his daughter. Inside the pages of her note was "a single sprig of Nevada sage-brush. Before I could protect myself, the memories were summoned up and washed over me in a flood." It smelled like home.

★ ★

The Magnet Lady
Henderson

Louise P. Greenfarb of Henderson is a hoarder. Since the 1970s, her passion has been refrigerator magnets. At last count, she had acquired more than thirty-five thousand nonduplicated magnets and earned a listing in the Guinness World Records for having the world's largest refrigerator magnet collection. For several years, about seven thousand of her magnets were displayed at the Las Vegas Guinness Museum (now closed). Known as the "the magnet lady," (her license plate is MGNTLDY), she started her collection by accident. When her children were young, they would often buy small magnets from vending machines. Worried that they might swallow the little metal and plastic objects, she began putting them on her refrigerator.

"From that time on, it became a growing hobby (or, as my family says, an obsession) that has never stopped to this day," she noted on her blog. Her husband was in the military, and the family moved all over the world, finding more magnets along the way. In 1989, she and her husband settled in Washington, where friends and others took notice of her collection. Soon, stories about her collection began appearing on television and in newspapers. In the early 1990s, she wrote to the Guinness World Records publishers to suggest she might have the world's largest collection of refrigerator magnets, but didn't qualify. In 1995, however, the editors reversed themselves and announced that she had made their list of world records.

Since then, she has made several national TV appearances, including Maury Povich's talk show, and worked as a consultant for—what else?—a South Korean magnet manufacturer, which wanted her to identify what type of magnets American consumers might purchase. Her collection includes cartoon figures, sexy magnets, plastic magnets, sports figure magnets, tourist trap magnets, and thousands of others. She also keeps about ten thousand duplicates that she uses for trading stock.

★ ★

And her search goes on. She continues to hunt for magnets at garage sales or as merchant giveaways. Since there's no more room on her refrigerator, she also attaches them to baking sheets. In 1997, she told the *Las Vegas Review-Journal* that when she dies, she hopes to be buried in her refrigerator, which would be covered with thousands of her favorite magnets.

One Man's Trash Is Another Man's Art

Imlay

Travelers on Interstate 80, between Lovelock and Winnemucca, often wonder about the bizarre, three-story concrete-and-glass structure that sits near the Imlay exit. Known as *Thunder Mountain Monument*, it is the work of self-taught environmental artist Frank Van Zandt, who often called himself Chief Rolling Mountain Thunder.

Born in Oklahoma in 1911, Van Zandt was a divinity school dropout who worked as a deputy sheriff and private investigator in northern California before arriving in Nevada in the mid-1960s. When his truck broke down in Imlay, he pushed it over to a spot beside the road and began living in it with his wife. He later said he had a vision telling him to move to the site, located in the shadow of Thunder Mountain, because it had spiritual qualities.

Once entrenched, he embraced a 1960s version of a Native American lifestyle, claiming he had Creek and Cheyenne blood. Then he opened a school that taught the fundamentals of living like Native Americans, and also began work on his creation.

Difficult to describe, and equally difficult to miss from the freeway, the work is without a doubt one of the most unusual folk art pieces in Nevada. Van Zandt erected it between 1969 and 1972, using whatever materials he could find because he said nothing should ever be wasted. So the monument is constructed of discarded tools, old bottles, auto parts, windshields, wood scraps, railroad ties, and

Thunder Mountain Monument—where one man's
junk became another man's artwork.
RICHARD MORENO

other found objects. The result is a conglomeration of weird stairways and ladders, spires, windows, arches, car axles, animal bones, bicycle parts, statues, and more. The artist also incorporated more than two hundred sculptures of faces and small human figures into walls, door-jambs, and surrounding trees.

The original monument consisted of eight separate buildings, including a hostel, studio, and general store. But a mysterious fire destroyed five of the structures and they were never rebuilt. Van Zandt committed suicide in 1989, but *Thunder Mountain Monument* is still owned by his family and is open to the public. In 1992, it was listed on the Nevada State Register of Historic Places.

What's in a Name?
Jiggs

Not many places can boast that they were named after a comic strip character. The settlement of Jiggs, however, not only can make that claim, but also holds the dubious record for changing its name almost as many times as Michael Jackson had plastic surgery.

The first white settler in the area was W. M. Kennedy, who established a small spread in 1866 and named the region Mound Valley (the largest landmarks were two big mounds). Three years later, David E. Hooten erected a way station on a new toll road through the valley and named it—surprise—Hooten Station. Then a nearby ranch became the area's first post office, and it was named Cottonwood. That post office closed shortly afterward, and another one, called Dry Creek, was established. Still later, the post office was relocated and the named reverted back to Mound Valley.

In 1884, a new post office named Skelton opened. That name stuck until around 1911, when merchant John Jesse Hylton bought most of the community's business places and petitioned to change the name to Hylton. In 1918, Hylton sold his holdings to Albert Hankins, who didn't want the previous owner's name on his town. So he listened when his children badgered him into naming the town Jiggs, after the

★ ★

main character in the then-popular comic strip *Bringing Up Father*. On December 18, 1918, the name was given formal approval.

The best place to hear about Jiggs's identity crisis is the Jiggs Bar, a small watering hole in the center of the tiny hamlet, which is located about thirty miles south of Elko via Route 227 and 228.

Underwater Ghost Town
Lake Mead

Every couple of decades, a forgotten community seems to rise out of Lake Mead. The town is (or was) St. Thomas, a Mormon farming settlement founded in 1865, which was submerged by lake waters after Hoover Dam was built in 1935. However, when the lake level drops, such as during extended drought periods, the ruins of St. Thomas reappear like some modern-day Atlantis.

Mormon farmers established St. Thomas at the confluence of the Muddy and Virgin Rivers in eastern Nevada. Because the Muddy River is fed by artesian springs, it was a reliable water source for growing crops. In the early 1870s, the Mormons abandoned St. Thomas as a result of a dispute with the state over taxes. The settlers had believed that their community was located in Utah, but an 1870 boundary survey showed it was within Nevada state lines. When Nevada sought two years of back taxes from residents, they returned to Utah. About a decade later, however, the Mormons began to come back to St. Thomas and soon the town again had several hundred residents.

The community thrived during the early part of the twentieth century, after the Union Pacific Railroad ran a branch line through the area and established St. Thomas as a terminus. During World War I, the town became an important shipping point for the local livestock industry as well as for copper mines in the region. Construction of Hoover Dam, however, spelled doom for St. Thomas. The dam's planners decided that the loss of a town was an acceptable trade-off for the project's benefits. The 224 residents (according to the 1930 census) were relocated to the nearby towns of Overton and Logandale. By 1938, St. Thomas was completely underwater.

But the walls and foundations reemerged. The first time was in the late 1950s, following a couple of dry years. Then the lake level rose and submerged it again, but St. Thomas kept reappearing. It happened in the late 1990s but the lake covered it again by the end of the millennium. Exceptionally dry years from 2002 to 2007 again dropped the water level, exposing the town once more. Wandering the site during the low-level periods provides glimpses of the old town. In addition to the concrete blocks and foundations, there are skeletal remains of trees.

Las Vegas Does Have a History
Las Vegas

There is something in Vegas that has been around longer than Wayne Newton. One of the original buildings of the Old Las Vegas Mormon Fort, the city's first settlement, can be found a few blocks north of downtown. Now a historic state park, the structure dates to 1855, although it has been changed and remodeled several times over the years.

In 1929, it was leased and renovated by the Bureau of Reclamation for use as a lab during the construction of Hoover Dam. The rectangular adobe structure now houses a small museum featuring displays and exhibits detailing the fort's history. Additionally, one of the rooms contains nineteenth-century furnishings—not originals—that show how the building most likely looked near the turn of the twentieth century.

The park also contains reconstructions of the fort's north and south walls, one of the bastions, the corrals, and a replica of the Pioneer Garden, complete with various crops like those planted 150 years ago.

The park is located at 500 East Washington Avenue, adjacent to Cashman Field and across the street from the Sawyer State Office Building. The park is open Tuesday through Saturday from 8 a.m. to 4:30 p.m., year-round. For information, call (702) 486-3511.

Where it all began in Vegas—the Old Mormon Fort
RICHARD MORENO

Cold War Reminder
Las Vegas

In the 1950s, getting bombed in Nevada didn't always involve alcohol. Between 1951 and 1992, nearly one thousand nuclear explosions were detonated at the Nevada Test Site, located sixty-five miles north of Las Vegas.

The first test, nicknamed "Abie," involved a B-50D bomber dropping a nuclear device from an altitude of 19,700 feet onto a barren patch of desert known as Frenchman Flat. The subsequent explosion

**The Atomic Testing Museum shows how Nevada's state
flower was once the mushroom cloud.**
PHOTO COURTESY OF THE ATOMIC TESTING MUSEUM

★ ★

generated a brilliant ball of rose-colored fire, followed by a blue-purple afterglow for a few seconds and a small, yellow-brown cloud that slowly drifted away until it was dissipated by the winds.

During the next four decades, the 1,375-square-mile test site (larger than Rhode Island and one of the largest restricted areas in the United States) hosted hundreds of nuclear detonations. In the early years, the blasts generated enormous mushroom-shaped clouds that rose high into the sky. Watching the scheduled tests became a popular tourist attraction, but after 1962 the tests were moved underground due to growing concern about fallout from the clouds.

The Atomic Testing Museum opened in Las Vegas in 2005. The eight-thousand-square-foot building, an affiliate of the Smithsonian Institution, is one of the first public museums devoted to the impacts of the Cold War. Inside, state-of-the-art displays describe the role that the Nevada Test Site had in the development of nuclear weapons, and the impact that "the bomb" had on American life.

Museum docents are often retired site workers who guide visitors through the galleries, which feature audio and video displays, test site artifacts, and items illustrating the public fascination with atomic tests during the 1950s. One classic example: a cereal box promoting the "Kix Atomic Bomb Ring."

The museum is located at 755 East Flamingo Road, and it's open Monday through Saturday from 10 a.m. to 5 p.m. and Sunday from 12 p.m. to 5 p.m. For more information, visit nationalatomictesting museum.org.

Kid Stuff for Grown-Ups
Las Vegas

The old children's game of rock-paper-scissors, also known as RoShamBo, has hit the big time. Once merely an amusing way for kids either to pass time or resolve differences, the venerable hand game is now the subject of national tournaments.

★ ★

In 2006, the Mandalay Bay Resort in Las Vegas hosted the inaugural USA Rock Paper Scissors Bud Light Finals. This competition, which was televised on the A&E cable network, attracted 260 of the best players in the country, who competed for a fifty-thousand-dollar first prize.

The rules are simple: Two contestants face off and at the count of three, present either a fist (rock), a flat hand (paper), or two fingers (scissors). Paper beats rock, rock beats scissors, and scissors beat paper. David McGill of Omaha, Nebraska, outlasted everyone to win the first competition.

But this isn't the only such tournament. The oldest is sponsored by the World Rock Paper Scissors Society, based in Toronto, Canada. The American version is this Nevada entry—the USA Rock Paper Scissors group, created by Hollywood producer Matti Leshem and supported by Anheuser-Busch, makers of Bud Light.

At the inaugural event, many contestants dressed in wacky and crazy costumes, ranging from a couple decked out as hot dog condiments to clones of Edward Scissorhands. And, not surprisingly given the main sponsor, most of the competitors consumed large quantities of beer before, during, and after.

For those who feel the need to try their hand at this age-old gesticulation game, the USARPS website (usarps.com) invites all comers to sign up for regional tournaments leading up to the big throwdown, held in Las Vegas each June.

Chew on This

Las Vegas

It was a match made in gastronomic heaven—one of the world's best-known brands of heartburn and indigestion relief products sponsored the world's largest buffet.

On March 28, 2006, Alka-Seltzer celebrated its seventy-fifth year of soothing upset tummies by sponsoring a 510-item buffet at the Las Vegas Hilton. The all-you-can-eat extravaganza, which set a

Guinness World Records record, included Mongolian chicken, salmon Wellington, cheese quesadillas, fajitas, barbecue beef ribs, fried chicken, tandoori chicken, soba noodle salad, bourbon-glazed ham, beef tenderloin tips braised in red wine, wood-roasted chicken breasts, tiramisu, New York–style cheesecake, and German chocolate cake.

Some twenty chefs and sous-chefs were on hand to present the dishes, which were accented by giant ice sculptures, including one in the shape of a huge "75," as well as an array of bubbling columns and other effervescent decor. George Bargisen, the Las Vegas Hilton's executive director of culinary operations, planned the menu and coordinated the event. He said his staff prepared 40 different soups; 149 types of dessert; 149 cold appetizers, salads, and sandwiches; and 152 hot items. In addition, there were ten carving stations to slice off slabs of roast beef, ham, and turkey, and five "action" stations, which were serving areas that prepared individualized servings of various pastas and desserts.

Open to the public, the event attracted 848 diners, each of whom paid a mere $7.50 for the opportunity to overindulge their way into history. All proceeds were donated to America's Second Harvest, the largest charitable hunger-relief organization in the United States.

Actress and comedienne Kathy Griffin served as hostess and took the first bite. The event was held in one of the hotel's largest ballrooms and covered more than 500 feet of combined table surface, spread across the 140-foot length of the room.

"Let's face it. I'm going to overindulge today and I'm going to pop a couple of Alka-Seltzer and then I'm going to be fine," Griffin joked during an interview just before the first forks were raised.

Fortunately for those who couldn't believe they ate the whole thing, Alka-Seltzer had relief stations scattered throughout the room serving up that familiar "plop, plop, fizz, fizz, oh what a relief it is" sound.

* *

"Howdy, Pardner"
Las Vegas

Since 1951, the massive neon and metal cowboy named Vegas Vic has greeted visitors to downtown Vegas. Standing forty feet tall, the illuminated buckaroo weighs about six tons and, at the time it was erected on top of the Pioneer Club, was the world's largest mechanical sign (his arm waved, his eye winked, and his cigarette moved and blew smoke rings).

Vic, who wears a cowboy hat and boots, blue jeans, a yellow checkered shirt, and a red bandana, was designed by Patrick Denner of Young Electric Sign Company (YESCO). Denner also created Wendover Will, a sixty-three-foot neon cowboy clone built in 1952 for the State Line Casino in West Wendover.

The design of Vegas Vic was based on an image that the Las Vegas Chamber of Commerce began using in the late 1940s, when the city was promoting itself with the slogan "Still a Frontier Town" (a far cry from Sin City's more recent "What Happens Here, Stays Here" advertisements).

In the mid-1950s, Vic began greeting passersby with a booming "Howdy, Pardner" message that was broadcast every fifteen minutes. But in 1966, according to local legend, actors Lee Marvin and Woody Strode were staying in the nearby Mint Hotel during the filming of *The Professionals* and complained that Vic's voice was annoying them. The owners of the Pioneer Club removed his voice box and didn't replace it for more than two decades. (Vic, however, went silent again in the 1990s. Maybe it was all those years of smoking neon cigarettes.)

The 1990s weren't a good time for the giant neon cowhand. By 1991, he had stopped waving his arm, supposedly because the club's owner at the time didn't like how it looked. In 1994, the construction of the Fremont Street Experience, a massive electronic canopy erected over several downtown blocks, necessitated the trimming of Vic's cowboy hat, which was chopped by a few feet. In January 2000, the *Las Vegas Journal-Review* reported, "Vic is in poor shape now. Only half

For more than a half century, the neon cowboy called
Vegas Vic has welcomed visitors to Glitter Gulch.
RICHARD MORENO

★ ★

his body, including one of his two eyes, lights up at night. His waving arm hasn't worked in years. His colorful clothes have faded and peeled."

Fortunately, later that year, Vic was given a long-overdue renovation. His sheet metal was repainted, mechanical parts were repaired, and neon tubing was patched and refilled with the electrified gases that give him his special glow.

Over his first half century, Vic has become one of the city's most endearing symbols. He has been described by *VIA* magazine as "Mr. Vegas," and has appeared in countless television commercials, music videos, and TV shows, as well as such films as *The Amazing Colossal Man*, *Viva Las Vegas*, *Diamonds Are Forever*, and *Casino*.

Vegas Vic can be seen standing atop the former Pioneer Club (it's now a souvenir shop) at 25 East Fremont Street.

One Whopping Big Nugget
Las Vegas

It just makes sense that if you have a hotel-casino and call it the Golden Nugget, you ought to have at least one golden nugget. The Golden Nugget hotel-casino did just that—except that its nugget is a staggering 875-troy-ounce hunk of gold (about sixty-one pounds, eleven ounces), the largest gold nugget on public display in the world.

Called "The Hand of Faith" because of its glovelike shape, the Golden Nugget's gold nugget was uncovered near Wedderburn, Victoria, Australia, in October 1980. It was found about six inches below the ground in a vertical position by a man using a metal detector. According to the Golden Nugget, "The Hand of Faith" is worth nearly $5 million. As an aside, the largest gold nugget ever recorded was a 172-pound specimen, known as the "Welcome Stranger." It was found in 1869, also in Victoria. It was melted down and produced about 156 pounds of pure gold.

Visitors to the Golden Nugget, located on Fremont Street, can view "The Hand of Faith" in the hotel's lobby. The hotel-casino traces its

★ ★

roots to 1946, when it became the first building in Sin City erected specifically for gambling. In 1973, Steve Wynn took over the aging property and transformed it from a Victorian/frontier-themed grind joint to a more classical hotel with lots of marble and shiny brass. More recently, it was purchased by the Landry Restaurants chain (owners of Landry's Seafood House, Rainforest Cafe, Chart House, and others), which remodeled the rooms, casino areas, and public space, including the big nugget display site. The new owners also added a giant pool with an aquarium, and revamped several restaurants.

Where Old Neon Goes to Die
Las Vegas

Think of the Las Vegas Neon Museum and its Neon Boneyard as a retirement home for old electric and neon signs. Many marquees and lighted signs end up in the junkyard, but a few are salvaged—some even restored—to become part of the museum or the Boneyard, as the storage area is known.

The museum is actually an outdoor display area at the entrance to the downtown Fremont Street Experience. It contains eleven restored, historic Las Vegas signs, including the Hacienda Horse and Rider, originally installed at the Hacienda Hotel in 1967; Aladdin's Lamp, a giant fairy tale–style neon lamp erected in 1966 in front of the Aladdin House; and the Chief Hotel Court sign, installed around 1940 at a former Las Vegas hotel.

Future plans call for the museum to have a visitor center, housed in the restored lobby of the historic La Concha Motel. The facility will sit at the entrance to the three-acre Boneyard at 821 Las Vegas Boulevard, near the Cashman Center. In 2006, the La Concha's one-thousand-foot lobby was dismantled and painstakingly moved from the southern end of the Strip to the Boneyard. The structure, which boasts a futuristic, swooping, shell-shaped roof, was built in 1961 and was designed by noted African-American architect Paul Revere

★ ★

The place where old neon is put out to pasture—
Las Vegas's Neon Museum's Boneyard
RICHARD MORENO

Williams, who was also responsible for the Beverly Hills Hotel and
the United Nations Building in Paris. It is considered a prime example
of the mid-twentieth-century modern roadside "Googie" style of
architecture.

The Boneyard, which is open only by appointment, offers an opportunity to wander through the oversize skeletons of many of the city's
most recognizable signs, including the Binion's Horseshoe marquee, the
high-heeled woman's shoe that once topped the Silver Slipper Casino,
and a curved Golden Nugget entrance sign. Most are in various states
of disrepair but the museum hopes to restore several of the icons.

★ ★

Many were built by the Young Electric Sign Company, which leased them to the establishments but retained ownership. When the signs were no longer wanted or needed, the company stored them for several years on its own property. A few years ago, they were relocated to the current museum site.

Tours of the Boneyard are available for large and small groups. For information on how to submit a tour request, go to neonmuseum.org.

Some New Mob Hits

Las Vegas

Since Las Vegas has more than one mobster as an integral part of its history, it's probably only natural that the city would also have more than one mob-related tourist attraction. And so it doés.

The first, known as the Las Vegas Mob Attraction, opened in 2011 in the Tropicana casino on the Strip, but shut down because of slow ticket sales and other problems. It was reopened in February 2012. On the eighty-third anniversary of the infamous St. Valentine's Day Massacre, the Mob Museum made its debut in a former Depression-era federal courthouse where the seventh of fourteen US Senate hearings on organized crime was held in the early 1950s.

The walls of one Mob Museum room are covered with bloody, uncensored photos of mob hits. In another, guests are shown how to load a gun, and then are exposed to other instruments of death the mobsters used to get rid of the opposition—things like a shovel, hammer, baseball bat, and ice pick. Also on display are tommy guns, money stacks, and a bullet-riddled brick wall from the 1929 massacre that elevated Al Capone to top dog of the Chicago mob.

The museum also attempts to trace the history of some of the more notorious gangsters. One photo shows Anthony "the Ant" Spilotro taking his First Communion; another features Frank "the Prime Minister" Costello lying in a hammock; a third is an image of Meyer Lansky and his daughter praying at the Western (Wailing) Wall in Jerusalem.

Naturally, there's a gift shop. One of the items for sale is a T-shirt that reads, "In Godfather We Trust."

The museum, located at 300 Stewart Avenue, is open daily. There's an admission charge. For details, call (702) 229-2734 or check out themobmuseum.org.

In the Mob Attraction (formerly the Las Vegas Mob Experience), visitors get access to the private lives of the likes of Ben "Bugsy" Siegel, Lansky, Spilotro, and many more through the use of interactive holograms, and live character actors who decide who gets invited into "the family." The attraction also features mob artifacts, memorabilia, photos, and videos.

The attraction is at 3801 Las Vegas Boulevard South. It's open daily, but it's not free. For details, call (702) 739-2662 or visit moblvdev.com.

Where Everybody Knows Your Name
McGill

The McGill Club is a funky, smoky, old-time watering hole that boasts a massive wooden back bar that is a century old—and dust that seems at least that old. But nobody goes to the McGill Club to admire its housekeeping. Folks stop in because the saloon has character and history, and because there aren't too many places like it in this world of cookie-cutter lounges and sports bars. For example, one of the highlights of a visit to the joint is viewing the patriotic display of photos of hundreds of local boys who have served in the military, including many dating back to World War II.

The impressive back bar, which was built in 1910 and transported to McGill via ship, train, and wagon, is among the club's most valuable assets. But part of the charm of the McGill Club is that, much like the town itself, nothing seems to change. A few decades ago, there might have been a few more open businesses, but overall it wouldn't appear much different from how it looks now. Perhaps that's because McGill, located twelve miles north of Ely via US Highway 93, was a company

Everyone will soon know your name if you stop
into the legendary McGill Club.
RICHARD MORENO

town. It was founded in 1906 and nearly everyone who lived there
worked for Kennecott Copper Corporation.

For the next fifty years, the town maintained a steady population
of around two thousand. But, as with all such towns, when the mines
closed, the jobs disappeared. This time it was in the early 1980s, when
Kennecott closed its eastern Nevada operations. In 1993, the company
cleared away the remains of the old smelter complex, including the
giant smokestack.

But the McGill Club is still around.

The Sole Tree
Middlegate

Travelers on US Highway 50 encounter an unusual sight—a giant cottonwood tree near Middlegate filled with pairs of hanging shoes. There are several versions of the story, but according to a 1998 Associated Press article, it started in the early 1990s when a young couple from Oregon went to Reno to get married. Fredda Stevenson, co-owner of a nearby saloon, told the AP reporter that as they camped out by the tree, they had their first big fight. The bride threatened to walk back to Oregon. But her new husband took her shoes, tied the laces into a knot and threw them up in the tree. "If you're going to walk home," he allegedly said, "you're going to have to climb a tree first."

The barkeep said the husband drove to her place and they talked. She convinced him to go back and apologize, and he did. A year later, they stopped by to show off their newborn child, whose first pair of shoes now hangs in the tree.

Over time, others saw the shoes in the seventy-foot-tall cottonwood and began tossing their own footwear into its branches. Now there are dozens of leather and canvas sneakers, oxfords, pumps, cowboy boots, wingtips, slippers, sandals, and other footgear hanging from the Old Shoe Tree.

A few years ago, an anonymous poet nailed a small, sock-shaped plaque to the tree. It reads, in part:

The Largest Shoe Tree in the world
My friend as you're driving by
Would you leave a pair of shoes
For now you have aplenty
So what have you to lose

The tree is located adjacent to US Highway 50, about 48 miles east of Fallon (about a mile east of the tiny outpost of Middlegate) or 110 miles east of Reno via US Highway 395 and US Highway 50.

A tree with a lot of sole—the Old Shoe Tree
RICHARD MORENO

The Lost Loot
Mogul

It's said that somewhere in the rolling hills west of Reno, near the community of Mogul, a small fortune in gold coins is hidden. Over the years, treasure seekers, some even armed with metal detectors, have tried unsuccessfully to find the trove, which supposedly includes some 150 twenty-dollar gold coins that today would be worth more than $250,000.

How the coins got there is an interesting historical tale. On November 5, 1870, five masked gunmen hijacked an eastbound Central Pacific train about six miles west of Reno. They stole about $41,800 in gold coins and silver bars, and then disappeared. Unfortunately for the criminals, the authorities were able to track down one of the robbers, who led them to his partners in crime. Eventually, everyone involved in the holdup was arrested and, except for two who testified against the others, sentenced to between five and twenty-three years in jail.

As far as anyone knows, however, the 150 gold coins are still out there somewhere. The crime has lived on in history because it's generally thought to be the first train robbery in the Far West. The transcontinental railroad line had been completed only about eighteen months earlier.

Nevada's Clay Cathedral
Panaca

In a state where the forces of nature have created some weird stuff, Cathedral Gorge rates a mention. Located a few miles north of Panaca, the gorge is a labyrinth of tall, deeply-grooved, tan-brown, bentonite clay spires and cliffs with a definite Gothic vibe.

They were created about a million years ago when much of this part of the state was underwater. Natural streams flowed into a large inland lake that covered the entire valley where the gorge is now located. Those streams also brought silt and clay that, over time, eventually filled the lake. Thousands of years later, the lake dried up and left behind a thick clay bed. Over the centuries, wind and rain eroded the clay, forming it into the evocative shapes found in the gorge today.

In the center of the formations, you feel as though you've been transported to another world. After climbing a set of wooden steps that leads to the northern entrance to the park, you reach a covered observation area known as the Miller's Point Overlook. From there, you

The famous churches of the world have nothin' on Cathedral Gorge.
RICHARD MORENO

can see almost the entire valley and admire the acres of marvelous clay sculptures.

The Nevada Division of State Parks has an attractive visitor center at Cathedral Gorge. It includes a small theater that shows videos describing the gorge and five other state parks in the region, and it's open throughout the year. The park has sixteen developed campsites with picnic tables, an RV dump station, toilets, and showers. They're open during the summer and fall. For more information, call (775) 728-4460.

Creative Financing

Pioche

Las Vegas didn't invent the skim or the kickback in Nevada. Both of these less-than-noble ways of doing business have been around for a long time. Just ask the people of Pioche.

In 1871, Pioche was an up-and-coming mining town that had a reputation for lawlessness. In fact, it was reported that some seventy-two men were buried in the cemetery before anyone actually died of natural causes. Seeing the need for some kind of justice, the town snagged the Lincoln County seat away from the tinier community of Hiko and decided to build a sturdy courthouse in which to hold trials and lock up the bad guys.

The project was budgeted to cost $16,400 but a year later, when the two-story stone structure was completed, the price had skyrocketed to about $88,000 because of cost overruns, money skimmed off the top, and kickbacks to suppliers.

Unfortunately for Pioche, this huge bill arrived just as the town of about seven thousand residents was entering a mining slump. The county was unable to pay for the building, so it did what governments usually do in such situations—it made minimal payments and borrowed more money. When those payments came due, the county was still unable to pay off the debt, so it refinanced the project, taking on additional interest.

★ ★

By the late 1880s, it's estimated that the amount due had risen to about $181,000. But the county just kept refinancing the debt. By the end of the century, Lincoln County owed more than $670,000 for its hall of justice. In fact, when the bill was finally settled in 1937, the county had shelled out nearly $1 million for the courthouse. Ironically, the building was condemned in 1933 and replaced in 1937 by a new courthouse, which was paid off on schedule and remains in use.

Despite its scandalous past, Pioche citizens took pride in their overpriced court structure and made efforts to preserve it. In recent years,

Pioche's Million Dollar Courthouse cost local residents a pretty penny.
RICHARD MORENO

the building has been renovated (for considerably less than $1 million) and reopened as a museum and art gallery. It is also used for community meetings and occasional theatrical performances.

Pioche is located about three and a half hours north of Las Vegas via Interstate 15 and US Highway 93. For more information, visit lincolncountynevada.com.

Shrine to Desperadoes
Primm

The bullet-riddled 1934 Ford V-8 looks a little out of place inside the modern rotunda that links the Primm Valley Resort to an outlet mall. The Cordoba gray classic sedan, however, is the Bonnie and Clyde Getaway Car, or Death Car, the vehicle driven by legendary outlaws Bonnie Parker and Clyde Barrow when they were ambushed and killed by law enforcement officials.

The story of Bonnie and Clyde is well documented (including the award-winning 1967 film *Bonnie and Clyde* with Warren Beatty and Faye Dunaway). The two met in West Dallas, Texas, early in 1930. Soon, they started a spree of bank robberies, kidnappings, burglaries, and murders throughout the South and Midwest. The FBI and other law enforcement agencies embarked on one of the largest manhunts in US history to capture the couple, who had gained national attention and become folk heroes.

Finally, on May 23, 1934, the duo was caught in an ambush on a rural road near Arcadia, Louisiana. Driving the stolen Ford V-8, they stopped to help the father of one of their gang members change a flat tire. Unbeknownst to the outlaws, the man and his flat were a ruse to distract Barrow and force him to drive to the side of the road closest to the waiting lawmen. As he climbed out of the car, the posse, consisting of six Louisiana and Texas officers, opened fire without warning, instantly killing Clyde. The group continued to fire bullets into the vehicle, in which Bonnie was sitting. It has been estimated that more than

★ ★

two dozen bullets were pumped into each body, as the officers emptied Browning automatic rifles, shotguns, and pistols during the assault.

After the two criminals were dead, the lawmen found that the car contained a small arsenal of weapons, including stolen automatic rifles, semiautomatic pistols, handguns, and thousands of rounds of ammunition.

The bullet-pocked Ford, which had been stolen from the Warren family of the nearby Bienville Parish in Louisiana, was eventually returned to its owners, who sold it to a carnival operator. It was shown around the country for several years before being placed on display in a Cincinnati theme park in the 1940s. In 1988, it was sold to Whiskey Pete's Casino, part of the Primm Valley Resort, located on Interstate 15 at the Nevada-California border. The casino's display shows the famous car, as well as historic photos of the Barrow family, the remains of the shirt Clyde was wearing when he died, his handmade mirror, and a belt and necklace he made while in prison.

The Truth Is Out There

Rachel

Perhaps no place in Nevada has captured the public's imagination as much as Area 51, also known as Dreamland or Groom Lake. Technically part of the Nevada Test Site, it's a 1,372-square-mile patch of desert where the nation has long tested its nuclear weapons.

And it's shrouded in mystery.

Though generally recognized as being a super-secret military air base, it has also been linked with extraterrestrial rumors, particularly those involving so-called unidentified flying objects (UFOs). According to Wikipedia, Area 51 "is not a conventional air base. . . . It instead appears to be used during the development, testing and training phases for new aircraft." However, the site adds, because the base is so secure, it is reportedly also home to a small number of Soviet-designed aircraft, which apparently are analyzed there and used for training exercises.

The ET Highway skirts Area 51, America's favorite alien conspiracy site.
PHOTO COURTESY OF THE NEVADA COMMISSION ON TOURISM

During the 1950s, Area 51 was used to test the U-2 spy plane and later for developing the SR-71 Blackbird, a high-speed reconnaissance plane. Since the late 1970s, the military has used the base for testing the prototypes for various "stealth" aircraft. Now there are rumors that work continues on the next generation of military planes, cruise missiles, supersonic spy planes, a stealth blimp, and a plane capable of flying in and out of space.

Some claim the UFO rumors are linked to the base's secretive operations and high-tech testing; others say the area has underground facilities that house such things as spaceships from other planets and the

★ ★

bodies of alien creatures. This notion has been advanced in the popular media and television shows like *The X Files.* One oft-circulated theory is that Area 51 is where the US government stored the flying saucer that allegedly crashed near Roswell, New Mexico, in the late 1940s.

Because of all the attention the area has received, in 1996 Nevada state tourism officials renamed the stretch of Route 375, which skirts the eastern edge of Area 51, as the "Extraterrestrial Highway." And the

Death of the World's Oldest Thing

In 1964, Donald R. Currey, a geology doctoral student at the University of North Carolina, was given permission by the US Forest Service to study the bristlecone pines growing in a grove at the base of Wheeler Peak in eastern Nevada. Currey was particularly interested in studying the rings inside these ancient trees, which had been discovered only a few years earlier. Researchers had identified bristlecones in the White Mountains of California as being as ancient as four thousand years old. Currey's research specialty was Ice Age glaciers, and he hoped that the bristlecone rings might provide some insights about the conditions of prehistoric times.

One of the trees in the Wheeler Park grove appeared to be extremely old, and it was Currey's desire to extract tree rings that could help him with his research. Most trees, including bristlecones, add a ring for each year they grow. Scientists study variations in the width of the rings to determine patterns of good and bad growing seasons over the years. The rings literally serve as a record of the lifetime of the tree, and are useful in the study of climate changes.

The Forest Service permitted Currey not only to take core samples from several of the oldest-looking trees, but also to cut down one of

★ ★

tiny town of Rachel (population one hundred) now promotes itself as the "official home of Area 51." A local business, the Little A'le'Inn, has a concrete time capsule it received from the production crew of the movie *Independence Day*, which was partially filmed in the area. The place also serves the "Beam Me Up Scotty," a stiff whiskey drink designed to have you talking to any aliens at the bar.

Bristlecone pines are older than most Las Vegas lounge acts.
PHOTO COURTESY OF THE NEVADA COMMISSION ON TOURISM

his choosing to examine its growth rings. Bristlecone pines grow in a kind of twisted way, which some- times makes it difficult to locate the oldest part of the tree in a core sample. The liv- ing one that Currey chose to remove, which later became known as "Prometheus," appeared to be a good can- didate. It was one of the largest and oldest-looking trees in the grove and seemed as though it would contain a large number of growth rings.

Although some of the Forest Service staff expressed reservations about cutting such an old tree, Currey was given the go-ahead, and the tree was cut down with a chain saw. Currey began counting the growth rings, which numbered about 4,900. Because every ring represents a year, it meant that the tree was nearly five thousand years old. Later, it was determined that Prometheus had been the oldest known living tree in the world.

At least it was until it was cut down.

★ ★

Place Setting for Twenty-Four
Reno

The Keck Museum, tucked inside the historic Mackay School of Mines on the University of Nevada–Reno campus, offers an eclectic mix of stones, fossils, mining equipment, and one very special silver set.

In 1876, mining millionaire John Mackay, who earned a fortune in Virginia City's mines, commissioned Tiffany & Company in New York to design and produce a silver service for his wife, Marie Louise. He shipped more than a half-ton of Comstock silver to the company and ordered it to make the "finest silver service possible." Charles Grosjean of Tiffany designed a 1,350-piece sterling silver dinner and dessert service for twenty-four diners. Two hundred silversmiths worked for two years (reportedly more than one million man-hours) to complete the set, which contains 14,718 ounces of silver.

Each piece bears Marie Louise's initials, MLM, and is decorated by hand in rich, floriated designs incorporating Irish shamrock, Scottish thistle, and American garden and wildflowers. Mackay purchased the casting dies used to make the service so that it could never be duplicated. The entire collection fit into nine walnut and mahogany chests, each mounted with a silver plaque detailing its contents.

In 1955, the Mackay family donated fifty-five pieces to the university, which has used them at important school events over the years. In the 1990s, the larger pieces were placed in the Keck Museum. They include an ornate silver soup tureen, a champagne cooler with a grape and vine design, and a pair of thirty-six-inch candelabra, the tallest ever made by Tiffany. The museum is open Monday through Friday from 9 a.m. to 4 p.m.

The Reno "Cure"
Reno

When its mining industry began to fade in the late nineteenth and early twentieth centuries, Nevada looked to other businesses to provide an economic boost. One of them was the divorce trade.

60

In 1906, Laura Corey, wife of William Corey, president of US Steel, relocated to Reno to take advantage of the state's liberal six-month residency requirement for obtaining a divorce. Her stay generated considerable publicity and established Reno as the place to get a quick divorce because other states required residency of at least one year. During the next few years, Reno gained an international reputation as a divorce factory for those who could afford it.

In 1927, legislators reduced the residency requirement to three months and, in 1931, dropped it to six weeks. As a result, by the 1920s and 1930s, Reno had become the *de facto* divorce capital of the world, and gossip columnist Walter Winchell dubbed it "getting

Newly divorced women are said to have tossed their old wedding bands into the Truckee River.
RICHARD MORENO

★ ★

a Reno-vation." Moreover, Nevada judges didn't require defendants to show cause, which avoided messy and ugly courtroom scenes. The rich and famous flocked to the city to take "the cure," and an entire divorce mill industry evolved. Those profiting included lawyers, hotels, motels, boardinghouses, and dude ranches that catered to the divorce-seekers. Between 1929 and 1939, an estimated thirty-two thousand marriages were abrogated in Reno.

Although Reno is no longer the numerical divorce capital of America (Las Vegas grabbed that crown long ago), it's still a popular choice for those wanting to untie the knot. According to the National Center for Health Statistics, Reno is still number one in terms of divorce rate, with 14.2 divorces per 1,000 residents. For anyone contemplating a Reno divorce, the Nevada State Bar Association has a fact sheet at nvbar.org/node/116; select "Divorce" to view the brochure.

Art Oasis
Rhyolite

In the early 1980s, the late Belgian artist Albert Szukalski, a renowned artist and sculptor in Europe, discovered the beauty of the Nevada desert. Drawn to the stark, open landscape, he moved to Beatty, Nevada, in 1984 and began working on *The Last Supper*, a surreal life-size creation of Leonardo da Vinci's painting of the same name that features ghostly silhouettes of Jesus and his apostles made from white plaster and fiberglass.

Szukalski recruited townspeople to pose in shrouds covered with hundreds of pounds of plaster. He said he created the work because the surroundings reminded him of Jesus's homeland in the Middle East. The work, built on top of a hill overlooking the ghost town of Rhyolite, was unveiled to little fanfare later that year. Within a short time, however, vandals had destroyed three of the figures, so Szukalski bought about eight acres on the edge of Rhyolite and relocated the figures to his property. He restored the original work, and then added other sculptures, such as *Ghost Rider*, a shrouded figure holding a

**Art needs fresh air and sunshine, too, as evidenced by the
Goldwell Open Air Museum.**
RICHARD MORENO

bicycle, and *Desert Flower*, a twisted mass of shiny chrome sprouting
from the ground. He also recruited other artist friends to join him in
creating an outdoor art gallery.

Within a few years, Szukalski's pieces were joined by several others,
including *Icara*, a giant wooden sculpture by Andre (Dre) Peters; Fred
Devoet's *Tribute to Shorty Harris*, a large metal outline of a prospector
and a penguin; and *Lady Desert: The Venus of Nevada*, a massive pink
cinderblock representation of a woman, by Dr. Hugo Heyman.

Following Szukalski's death in 2000, his outdoor sculpture garden and land were donated to the Goldwell Open Air Museum,

which maintains the works and develops art programs. The museum is located about four miles west of Beatty, on the road leading to Rhyolite. For more information, log on to goldwellmuseum.org.

Bottoms Up
Rhyolite

The desert around Rhyolite is barren and dry. There are no trees and few shrubs. So, when it came to building materials, residents were forced to get creative—like saloon owner Tom Kelly, who built a three-room house using an estimated thirty thousand empty beer bottles, held together with adobe. According to the Friends of Rhyolite, a local preservation group, it took Kelly a little less than six months to construct the unusual home, which was completed in February 1906.

The Adolphus Busch Company (today known as Budweiser) manufactured nearly all the bottles, which apparently were acquired from the several dozen saloons that operated in the area. Based on the condition of some of the bottles, it appears that Kelly didn't wash them before putting them to a new use.

Kelly was seventy-two when he built the house. He abandoned it six years later, most likely because the Rhyolite mining boom was over. In 1925, Paramount Pictures discovered the town and the quaint bottle house, and featured it in a silent film, *The Air Mail*, starring Warner Baxter, Billie Dove, and Douglas Fairbanks Jr.

In the mid-1950s, Tommy and Mary Thompson and their children occupied the house and operated it as a museum and rock house. When his parents died, their son Evan maintained the property until about 1989. The Bureau of Land Management assumed responsibility for the structure in 1990. By then it needed significant restoration because a large hole had developed near a gable and the wall had begun to collapse. The building therefore underwent a significant reconstruction process that included replacing the roof and shingles, adding bracing for the walls and roof, and rebuilding the front porch.

The Rhyolite Bottle House is one of Nevada's earliest recycling projects.
RICHARD MORENO

These days, the bottle house is one of the best-looking structures in the ghost town, and is always included on volunteer-led guided tours. For more information, go to rhyolitesite.com.

Wovoka and the Ghost Dance

Schurz

There's a grave in the Paiute Cemetery in Schurz (located about one hundred miles southeast of Reno) with a headstone much larger than those around it. It's the grave of Jack Wilson, also known as Wovoka,

Paiute Messiah Wovoka sparked the
Ghost Dance Indian religious movement.
RICHARD MORENO

the Paiute Messiah. In the late nineteenth century, he was the leader of a Native American religious movement known as the Ghost Dance, which, for a time, swept the Indian nation.

The Ghost Dance encouraged followers to be good to others, to cease hostilities with whites, and not to steal. By doing those things and regularly engaging in a frenzied five-day dancing ritual, participants were told they'd go to a place with no sickness, death, or disease, and be reunited with ancestors and loved ones who had died.

Wovoka was born in Yerington, Nevada, in 1856. In 1887, he had a vision that told him how to help the Indian people achieve a happy afterlife. He began preaching to local tribes, and word of his new religion spread. But as the movement evolved, it moved away from its source. Soon, some followers proclaimed that the dance would make all whites disappear, while others began wearing "ghost shirts," which they believed would make them bulletproof.

The movement came to a tragic end at Wounded Knee, South Dakota, in December 1890 when US Army troops opened fire on a crowd of Lakota Sioux who were participating in the Ghost Dance. The soldiers launched the attack because they believed the Sioux were preparing an attack. The great chief Sitting Bull and 150 others, mostly women and children, were killed. The massacre hastened the end of the movement, although Wovoka continued to be a revered spiritual leader for the rest of his life. He died in Yerington in 1932.

What's in a Name?
Searchlight

Depending on which version of the story you hear, the old mining town of Searchlight, located fifty-five miles south of Las Vegas on US Highway 95, was named after a popular brand of wooden matches, in honor of a miner named Lloyd Searchlight, or by one of the town's earliest prospectors, who allegedly quipped that it would take a searchlight to find any gold in the region.

Searchlight may or may not have been named after a box of matches.
RICHARD MORENO

★ ★

All three stories have appeared in various history books over the years. However, one of the town's native sons, US Senator Harry Reid, born in Searchlight in 1939, has written a history of his hometown and concluded that the latter tale is most likely the truth.

In his book *Searchlight: The Camp That Didn't Fail*, Reid reveals that he could find no evidence of any miner named Lloyd Searchlight. It also appears that the tale of the town being named after the Searchlight brand of wooden matches was most likely the fanciful concoction of a descendant of one of the town's founders. Reid's research did show, however, that Searchlight probably got its name when one of the town's first residents, prospector George Colton, remarked that there was gold in the area but it would take a searchlight to find it.

The town traces its beginnings to about May 1897, with the discovery of gold in the area. Within a year, a mining district had been formed and a small tent camp cropped up in the desert. By 1907, Searchlight had a population of several thousand, stores, saloons, a post office, a newspaper, and a fifteen-mile-long narrow gauge railroad. But the ore began to fade and by 1930, the census counted only 137 residents. Today, about one thousand people live there, away from the hustle of the big cities.

The Land of the Mutant Rocks
Valley of Fire State Park

There are some strange stones at Valley of Fire State Park. One, called Elephant Rock, resembles a pachyderm with thick legs and a long trunk. In another part of the park are the Beehives, several large round sandstone formations scored with concentric cracks and lines that make them resemble stone hives. And then there are the Seven Sisters, a row of massive red sandstone pillars; Piano Rock, which looks like an upright piano; Poodle Rock, which bears strong resemblance to that canine's distinctive head; and Duck Rock, which, of course, takes after a duck.

★ ★

The park is also home to a significant collection of prehistoric petroglyphs. Geologists say that erosion created this sandstone sculpture
garden. The sandstone traces its origins to about 150 million years
ago, when the area was largely shifting sand dunes. The sand eventually turned into stone, which over the centuries has been carved by the
wind and rain into such a wide variety of evocative shapes. The distinctive red-colored sandstone is the result of oxidized iron that permeated
the rock.

Archaeological evidence indicates that the valley has long attracted
people. Among the earliest inhabitants were the Basketmaker people

Weird formations can be found at Valley of Fire State Park.
PHOTO COURTESY OF THE NEVADA COMMISSION ON TOURISM

★ ★

and the Anasazi Pueblo farmers from the nearby Moapa Valley. Proof of their presence can be found among the many petroglyphs (prehistoric rock writings) on the valley walls. In Petroglyph Canyon north of the visitor center, the walls are lined with such glyphs as rare kachinas, dancers, footprints, and curved lines.

The visitor center offers exhibits and displays about the geology and animal life of the region, including the rare and protected desert tortoise, plus good information about desert flora and fauna. The park also has two campgrounds with fifty campsites. It is located about fifty miles northeast of Las Vegas. For information, call (702) 397-2088.

Virginia City's Lively Ghosts
Virginia City

For years, Virginia City billed itself as "the West's Liveliest Ghost Town," so it's logical that the former mining community would be the focus of many ghost stories. Reportedly, specters have been seen in about a dozen places in the city, and two books have been written about the subject.

Among the ghost-sighting sites is St. Mary's Art Center, housed in the former St. Marie Louise Hospital. It was built in 1876 and was operated for decades by the Sisters of Charity. These days, witnesses have reported seeing a woman in a long white robe, or a nun dressed in white robes, roaming the hallways and looking out the windows of the structure. One version of this story is that in 1878, a patient in the psychiatric ward started a fire that killed him and a nun. Now she allegedly wanders the building looking for patients to help, and frequently musses the sheets and blankets on the bed in her former room.

There have also been reports of a blonde-haired female ghost, affectionately known as Lena, on the spiral staircase near the back of the Old Washoe Club Bar. Opened in the 1870s, it was originally known as the Millionaires Club, a drinking establishment for the most successful businessmen. There have also been sightings of an old prospector sitting at one of the barstools, as well as the ghost of a thirteen-year-old girl who some believe was murdered in an upstairs bedroom.

Beware of the ghostly nun said to haunt
St. Mary's Art Center.
RICHARD MORENO

Other sightings have occurred in the city's Silver Terrace Cemetery, where people claim to have witnessed a strange glowing tombstone at night, and at the Fourth Ward School in South Virginia City, allegedly home to "Miss Suzette," a ghost who walks across the schoolyard. Others have reported seeing the ghost of Henry Comstock, one of the founders of Virginia City and namesake of the Comstock Lode. According to local ghost lore, Comstock committed suicide in 1870 but now has returned to reclaim the holdings he allegedly sold for a mere eleven thousand dollars, far less than they were worth.

Racing Camels and Mobile Commodes
Virginia City

Each fall, Virginia City holds two unique races. One involves smelly, ill-tempered, spitting camels. The other features non-smelly outhouses on wheels.

The annual camel races, held over three days in early September, draw twenty-five thousand to thirty thousand spectators, all eager to see whether the jockeys can manage to hang on to the untrained beasts long enough to finish the hundred-yard dashes on a straight dirt track. Over the years, organizers have also added races with other exotic animals, including ostriches, emus, and bulls. Periodically, riders from Australia, where camel races are also popular, compete for a four-foot-tall trophy called the International Camel Cup.

The camel races started as a joke in 1959 when Bob Richards, editor of Virginia City's *Territorial Enterprise*, published the results of local camel races, even though there had been no such races. He concocted the idea because in the early 1860s, Virginia City had been home to a couple of camel freight operations.

Although his story didn't get much reaction from the locals who were accustomed to his sense of humor, the editors of the *San Francisco Chronicle* picked it up. A year later, Richards again announced the nonexistent event but this time, the *Chronicle* responded by announcing that it had hired several camels and was challenging all comers. Not to be outdone, the *Phoenix Gazette* and

★ ★

Spit happens at the annual Virginia City International Camel Races.
PHOTO COURTESY OF THE NEVADA COMMISSION ON TOURISM

the Indio, California, Chamber of Commerce accepted the challenge
and suddenly the fictitious race became a reality.

The San Francisco Zoo provided camels and Hollywood director
John Huston was brought in as a "ringer" rider to publicize the race.
He beat all comers and the race became an annual event.

Even more unusual are the World Championship Outhouse Races,
held the first weekend in October. Since the early 1990s, the oddball
competition has attracted a wide variety of mobile outhouse designs and
shapes, many built specifically for the races. The winner of the double-
elimination event receives the Royal Flush Trophy, which is shaped like

a glass outhouse. Runners-up get toilet seats and bedpans. According to the organizers, the races are in honor of Virginia City's colorful past, when the county banned the use of outhouses in the town, leading many residents to put theirs on wheels and parade them on the main street. In recent years, winners have coasted to victory in mobile privies with names like "The Urinator," "Stool Shed," and "Flaming Butt Hut."

For more information on either event, contact the Virginia City Tourism Commission, (800) 718-7587, or go to visitvirginacitynv.com.

The Mountain Oyster Fry
Virginia City

Sometimes, there is just no accounting for taste. Literally. While some towns are content to host simple rib cook-offs or chili contests, Virginia City is home to the annual Mountain Oyster Fry, which most locals prefer to call "the Testicle Festival."

Each March, teams of contestants, known as "gonadologists," cook up sheep testicles in a variety of dishes. Started in 1991, the event attracts as many as two dozen teams of cooks from around the country who prepare tasty testicular treats. The rules are pretty simple: Each team must cook up at least twenty pounds of mountain oysters, and all cooking must be done in the parking lot of the Bucket of Blood saloon, without the advantage of electrical plug-ins. Chefs can prepare them in any style, using any sauce or garnish.

A panel of judges samples the creatively concocted cojones and pronounces winners in such categories as best overall taste, most creative use of flavors, best booth, best first-time cook, and best presentation. The event attracts about twelve thousand spectators, many of whom wander the booths and sample the wares. Reflecting the flavor of the cook-off, many teams adopt colorful names, such as "Clammy Balls," "Galletti's Gonads," "Great Balls of Fire," and "the McCastrate Sisters." Dishes have included oyster po' boys, Eunuch Nachos, lamb nut chowder, and coconut curry balls.

Yum.

★ ★

For more information about this delectable happening, contact
the city's Convention and Tourism Commission at (800) 718-7587, or
check out visitvirginiacitynv.com.

Historic Graffiti

Wendover

At the start of World War II, the US military opened the Wendover
Bombing and Gunnery Range in the desert flats outside Wendover.
Over the next several years, the facility expanded as additional

**The graffiti on the rocks above Wendover is actually considered
historic, with much of it dating back to World War II.**
RICHARD MORENO

★ ★

companies of troops were sent there for training. In 1944, Wendover was selected to be the training ground for the 509th Composite Group, a top-secret contingent of troops that trained and prepared to drop an atomic bomb on Japan. On August 6, 1945, the group's commander, Colonel Paul Tibbets Jr., piloted the *Enola Gay*, which dropped the device on Hiroshima, Japan, effectively ending the war.

During their time at Wendover, bored airmen and soldiers began painting the giant rocks and cliffs overlooking the area with messages and images, including the numerical insignias of the various troop companies. The graffiti has long been considered an eyesore, but in recent years historians have begun to view the painted white letters and drawings as an important snapshot of that era.

The Fibbing Festival
Yerington

In the nineteenth century, it was sometimes difficult to tell the truth from fiction in many Nevada newspapers. Fabricated stories—including many by humorist Mark Twain—were tradition among the publications. In fact, in 1873, the editor of Austin's newspaper, *The Reese River Reveille*, concocted stories about the Sazerac Lying Club, a nonexistent social club dedicated to telling lies.

The editor, Fred Hart, described the election of officers—all real people living in Austin—and shared a few colorful lies allegedly told during the first meeting. The response was so positive that for months afterward, the paper entertained readers with tales of the wild lies and outrageous claims made by club members during their regular meetings. Soon, other western newspapers picked up the articles, and eventually Austin's famed fibbing club was the subject of a book containing Hart's articles. The joke came to an end in 1877, when Hart left the paper and moved to Virginia City. He wrote a final story about the club's dissolution, thereby ending the existence of a club that never existed.

But in 2006, the town of Yerington decided to resurrect the idea. On April Fools Day of that year, the community hosted the Occasional Lyon County Liar's Contest. The event attracted more than one hundred people, who listened to tall tales about ghosts, animals, fish, and other subjects. The judges included a local judge and a brothel madam; the winner was a candidate for sheriff. He lost the election.

2

Arizona

Perhaps the vast *majority of those who call Arizona home did not originate here. But, as I've discovered while rambling around the state and writing three editions of* Arizona Curiosities *for Globe Pequot Press over the past decade, that's a good thing, curiosity-wise. Because of the diversity of backgrounds, the immigrants brought with them some pretty good idiosyncrasies and that's what books like this are all about.*

So a curiosity-seeking odyssey across Arizona leads to deserts, libraries, mountain ranges, museums, visitor and historical centers, and yes, even an occasional saloon. The excursions result in encounters with people who paint big rocks to resemble green frogs and bleached spooky skulls; people who create weird icons made of concrete, steel, and plaster; and a countless number of people who, when asked if there was anything weird in their town, inevitably replied, "Yep, and you're lookin' at one of 'em."

The journey uncovers golf courses with rules for meeting up with rattlesnakes, Christmas trees composed of tumbleweeds, homes that were once granaries, artists who used boulders and block walls as their canvases, and a centennial building covered with street signs.

Those who take the time to make such oddity-seeking treks will find a church that seats only six, a Greek monastery in the Sonoran Desert, a series of lighthouses illuminating the desert, a peace symbol made of

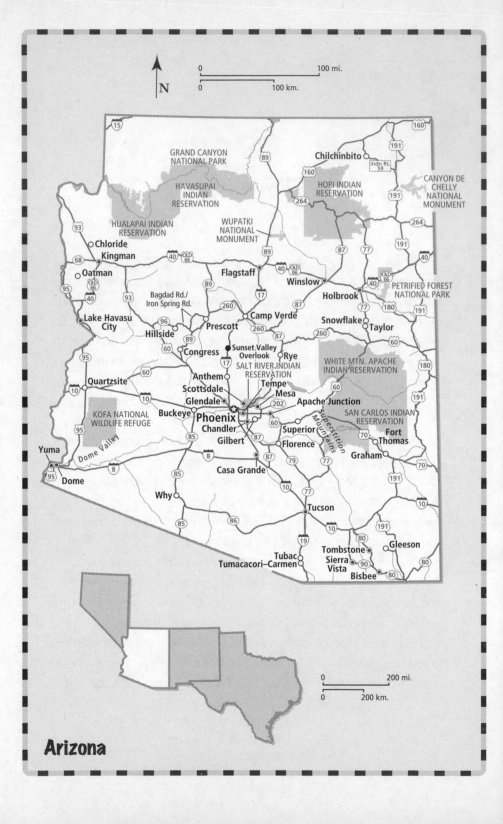

N

0 ___ 100 mi.
0 ___ 100 km.

GRAND CANYON
NATIONAL PARK

HAVASUPAI
INDIAN
RESERVATION

HUALAPAI INDIAN
RESERVATION

Chilchinbito

Indn Rt.
59

HOPI INDIAN
RESERVATION

CANYON DE
CHELLY
NATIONAL
MONUMENT

WUPATKI
NATIONAL
MONUMENT

Chloride
Kingman

Oatman

Lake Havasu
City

Hillside

Bagdad Rd./
Iron Spring Rd.

Prescott

Flagstaff

Camp Verde

Winslow

Holbrook

Snowflake
Taylor

PETRIFIED FOREST
NATIONAL PARK

Sunset Valley
Overlook

Congress

Rye

WHITE MTN. APACHE
INDIAN RESERVATION

SALT RIVER INDIAN
RESERVATION

Quartzsite

Anthem

Scottsdale

Glendale

Buckeye

Tempe
Mesa

Apache Junction

SAN CARLOS INDIAN
RESERVATION

KOFA NATIONAL
WILDLIFE REFUGE

Phoenix

Chandler

Gilbert

Superior

Florence

Superstition
Mountains

Fort
Thomas

Graham

Yuma

Dome

Dome Valley

Why

Casa Grande

Tucson

Tombstone
Gleeson

Tubac

Sierra
Vista

Bisbee

Tumacacori–Carmen

Arizona

⭐ ⭐

recycled guns, an obelisk rising out of the desert sands, and a curse that follows petrified-wood thieves. They'll learn which corner to stand on along Route 66, how to test for vertigo while looking down into the Grand Canyon, and where to find milkshakes with a royal history.

Also, they can eat fry bread at a roadside stand, stand in four states at the same time, drive across roads that were seemingly laid out by a snake with hiccups, sleep in a reconstituted travel trailer, and visit a school with planetary designs.

It's all pretty much weird, and it's all here, in curious Arizona.

★ ★

A Solar Tribute
Anthem

Anthem's Veterans Memorial is impressive, touching, and monumental, hardly the requisites for inclusion in a compilation of oddities. It is composed of five large marble pillars of varying lengths, standing in perpendicular perfection about two feet apart. Each has an angled circle cut through the stone, and the pillars are so well aligned that the circles form a downward channel.

The Anthem Veterans Memorial honors those who have served in the military in a unique manner.

The pillars represent the five branches of the United States military, staggered in size and ordered in accordance with the Department of Defense prescribed precedence. The Army pillar is the tallest; the Coast Guard's the shortest. In between are the Marine Corps, Navy, and Air Force.

The memorial's original proposal came from Anthem resident Ron Tucker, a retired rear admiral; it was designed by Renee Palmer-Jones, also of Anthem.

But on to the curious parts.

First, every November 11, Veterans Day, at exactly 11:11 a.m., the sun shoots a beam through the channel and casts a circular light on a mosaic representation of the Great Seal of the United States. It's a spectacular combination of architecture and astronomy.

Second, every aspect of the project—from design to engineering to fundraising—was done by local volunteers.

The memorial, which was designated as a historic site by the Arizona Historical Society in 2012, is located in the Anthem Community Park, 41703 N. Gavilan Parkway. For more information, visit onlineatanthem.com/anthem-veterans-memorial.

The Snake Hole Golf and Country Club

Apache Junction

There are almost two hundred golf courses listed for the metropolitan Phoenix area. The Snake Hole Golf and Country Club isn't on the list, however, because its members march to a different five-iron.

It's not a long course, at nine holes, par 29. The first hole is a tricky little eighty-nine-yarder that crosses creosote bushes, open desert, and the exact spot where one member said he saw a rattlesnake. Like all the others, the first green is small and brown because it's sand, not grass. This is not unusual at Snake Hole. There's no grass. Anywhere.

The course sits on five acres of leased desert. Membership is restricted to residents of the Countryside RV Resort, located directly across the road so members don't have to put a lot of miles on their golf carts getting there. Because the entire course is sand, there's no need for sand bunkers. No grass bunkers, either.

The greens are a darker shade of brown than the fairways because they're oiled sand. This holds the putting surfaces down when the wind blows. The members are mostly winter visitors on limited budgets so they're also the greenskeepers. This means they have to find their own used oil. Some of it comes from fast-food restaurants, which sometimes leads to the question, "Would you like fries with that double bogey?"

Sand golfers also allow "stands." The ground is so hard they can't use regular tees even if they try to whack them into the arid soil with a driver, so they stand their ball on a little three-legged plastic gizmo before hitting it. And they get to "stand" their ball on every shot, not just on the tee boxes. Another deviation is the rattlesnake rule. If you see a rattler, you get to pick up your ball and subtract as many strokes from your score as you think necessary to get your heart rate back to normal.

The course is on Idaho Road just north of the Superstition Freeway, but don't go there expecting to lower your average just because none of the holes is longer than one hundred yards. You need a membership to play.

Home Is Where the Airstream Is
Bisbee

The Shady Dell Trailer Court is neither shady nor delled. It is, instead, a sort of museum that exists primarily to prove the theorem that if somebody collects something, somebody else will come to look at it. Or, in this case, to stay in it.

The collection is old travel trailers, those aluminum tag-alongs that date as far back as the 1930s. Ed Smith and Rita Personett started it in 1955 when they bought a homemade unit and hauled it back to Bisbee from California. They soon acquired two more and bought a trailer park, which they renamed the Shady Dell.

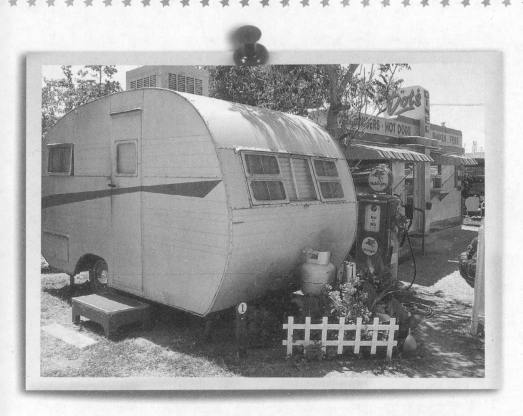

Need a good night's sleep in a tin trailer? The Shady Dell Trailer Court in Bisbee offers accommodations in restored travel trailers, plus meals at Dot's Diner.

At first, Smith didn't look at the acquisitions as a financial venture. He planned to restore the trailers and put them on display as an art project. But Personett saw it as a business endeavor, so they cleaned up the trailers they already had, bought a few more, and offered them as guest houses. They also purchased an old diner that now serves as an eating spot and gathering place for their clientele.

Smith and Personett operated the park until they sold it to Laura Chumley and Wesley Barchenger, who added a 1957 Airfloat and a 1957 Airporter bus that has been transformed into a "Polynesian palace." In 2007, the couple sold the establishment to Justin Luria and his mother, Annette, who have added more trailers, more plastic flamingos, and some artificial grass. Now guests can choose from a 1949 Airstream, a '57 El Rey, or a '51 Spartan Mansion. Or rest up in a cabin cruiser sitting on blocks, or sleep in an old bus. Each unit has been painstakingly restored, from the Melmac dishes in plywood cupboards, to the dial radios sitting on Formica countertops, to the knick-knacks on the walls.

If sleeping in cramped quarters is your kind of fun, log on to theshadydell.com or call (520) 432-3567. Reservations are required.

The Concrete Metal Man
Bisbee

In November 2010, residents of Bisbee staged a major celebration to honor the seventy-fifth anniversary of a statue.

The sculpture is a Bisbee icon. It stands nine feet tall, weighs a ton, and is affectionately called both "the Iron Man" and "the Copper Man" by the local citizenry. But the official name is the Courthouse Plaza Miners' Monument because it stands in the Cochise County courthouse plaza and is a tribute to the city's mining heritage.

Since 1877, Bisbee mining enterprises have removed eight billion pounds of copper, 102 million ounces of silver, and 2.8 million ounces of gold from the surrounding landscape. The statue honoring those numbers was completed in 1936, and was the first major commission for local artist Raymond Phillips Sanderson. The bare-chested Art Deco figure represents a stalwart miner wearing pants and boots, and holding the tools of his trade. Lee Petrovitch, a local resident, served as the model for the work because, according to the artist, "his finely proportioned physique was ideally suited to the undertaking."

But although it's a miner representing the mining industry, the statue isn't composed of either copper or iron. It's concrete, covered with copper plating. Sanderson utilized what was then a new technique and nearly two hundred pounds of copper wire. The wire was fed through an oxyacetylene-heated gun and sprayed under pressure to coat the cement. The work stands on the corner of Tombstone Canyon and Quality Hill.

Bisbee's iconic Iron Man isn't really iron.
He's concrete covered with copper plating.

The Hobo Who Survived
Buckeye

When he was at the peak of his career, Hobo Joe stood tall and beckoned the hungry to dine at a local eatery bearing his name. He was one of several large fiberglass figures that were spread across the country back in the 1960s to advertise the Hobo Joe chain.

He may not be welcome in town, but Hobo Joe stands tall and keeps smiling.

However, when the restaurant chain went out of business, the giant Hobo Joes were left destitute. Many of them were destroyed. But the one in Buckeye survived, although it became the object of scorn and the subject of a citywide controversy.

California artist Jim Casey created the sculpture. Buckeye resident Marvin Ransdell owned the fiberglass plant that cast the local version from Casey's original. The twenty-five-foot sculpture came back into Ransdell's possession when the restaurant closed. When Ransdell died, he willed it to Ramon Gillum, a close friend. Gillum asked that the work be resurrected and placed in the downtown area, but his request met stiff local opposition because many residents didn't think an over-size tramp was a fitting symbol for their community.

Frustrated, Gillum decided to keep the statue for himself. After getting the necessary approval from the city, he moved Hobo Joe onto his own property, a meat-processing plant on the eastern outskirts of the city where it stands today. It is only one of two such artworks left in the country, Gillum told city officials during the commotion.

Now it rises on a pedestal at the east end of Buckeye at the intersection of Monroe Street and Apache Road, and extends a cheerful salute to all those who pass by. A plaque at the base dedicates it to Ransdell's memory

The Call of the Kokopelli
Camp Verde

The kokopelli—or the flute player—is a fertility symbol among the Hopi Indians, but the image doesn't always have cultural significance. For example, there's a huge kokopelli here that stands perpetual watch over such treasures as plaster Tweety Birds, plastic snakes, Arizona-themed T-shirts and ball caps, and a replica of *Venus de Milo*. It performs this function at the Krazy Kokopelli Trading Post, a tourist-oriented establishment that offers for sale, among other things, bumper stickers that read LOTTERY: A TAX ON PEOPLE WHO ARE BAD AT MATH and HAPPINESS IS AN EMPTY HOLDING TANK.

**The world's largest kokopelli welcomes tourists
and bargain hunters at Camp Verde.**

Despite that wealth of merchandise, the kokopelli is probably the main reason most people stop. This is understandable. The sculpture stands thirty-two feet tall, is painted bright yellow, and is perched on a six-foot base, so it readily dominates the skyline.

Lowell Johnson, one of the store owners when the statue was built and erected, said it's the world's largest kokopelli and that nobody ever challenged the claim. The big musician is made of welded steel, cost twenty-five thousand dollars, and weighs five and a half tons. It was created by the father-son combo of Gerry Berg Sr. and Gerry Berg Jr., who spent about forty-five days working on the project.

Flute players and fertility seekers can see the giant just off Interstate 17 at Camp Verde.

These Domes Are Nobody's Homes
Casa Grande

Snoopy folks who like to wander the back roads in search of things of an unusual nature are likely to have their curiosity glands shift into overdrive when they come across the relics squatting on a barren plot of Sonoran Desert south of Casa Grande. At first glance, it looks like a place where UFOs come to die. Or a final resting place for huge alien creatures. But closer inspection reveals that it's man-made, and it's spooky.

The piece of desert is covered by a series of concrete domes. Some stand (or squat) alone. Others are connected so they resemble a giant, but very dead, caterpillar. They're all abandoned and have been severely vandalized, so there are no doors or windows left. Only big round things, just squatting there, staring vacantly and forlornly at the hostile landscape that surrounds them.

The basic domes were constructed of concrete, and then covered with a chemical foam. They were built to house a projected electronics circuit board factory, but the project never materialized and the site was abandoned. Now it is utilized primarily by underage beer drinkers, graffiti artists equipped with an apparently never-ending supply of spray paint, and an incessant wind that screeches a frightening howl through the emptiness.

And, according to some, a community of ghosts also has taken up residency, and they shriek with other-worldly eeriness designed to keep the tourists away.

The site is on the east side of Thornton Road, 1.1 miles south of Interstate 8.

Creosote Bush: A Killer?

In the Desert

Anyone who has ever wandered into any Arizona desert has undoubtedly encountered a rather plentiful, scruffy-looking plant known as the creosote bush.

They're not very eye-catching because they're spindly shrubs that stand anywhere from three to six feet tall and measure about two to ten feet across. The stems carry small resinous leaves and, in the spring, they bear little yellow flowers. But that undistinguished exterior conceals a long-living plant with deadly instincts.

Although the bushes grow in somewhat orderly patterns across the desert, much like man-made orchards, there's a reason for the spacing. For a long time, botanists thought it was because the creosotes had the ability to grow poisonous shoots that killed any other plant trying to take root in its territory. That's only partially true. They do have the ability to produce chemicals that inhibit the growth of certain others.

But now, scientists believe that the root systems of the mature creosote bushes are so efficient at absorbing water that there's none left for any other seeds, so they can't germinate. Either way, nobody messes with creosotes when it comes to protecting their territory.

And here are a couple of other creosote noteworthies: First, they can live a long time. One grouping in the Mohave Desert of California has been around for an estimated 11,700 years. Second, despite the name, they don't produce the tar-like creosote used to preserve railroad ties. That smelly stuff comes from a certain variety of pine tree.

* *

O Tumbleweed, O Tumbleweed
Chandler

The city of Chandler may be the only one in the nation that faces a shortage of the materials required to put up a Christmas tree. Blame it on housing developments and the population explosion.

Every year since 1957, the city has erected a Christmas tree composed entirely of tumbleweeds, chicken wire, and spray paint. Starting

Chandler's annual Christmas tree requires hundreds of tumbleweeds and gallons of white paint.

in mid-November, the wire is shaped into a thirty-foot cone, and more than one thousand dried tumbleweeds are inserted into the holes. Then work crews cover the faux tree with twenty-five gallons of white paint, twenty gallons of flame retardant, and sixty-five pounds of glitter. As the final touch, they also install about twelve hundred lights.

But tumbleweeds are getting harder to come by. New houses now cover much of the land that once served as prime tumbleweed acreage, and nonagricultural property owners who are waiting to sell their land to developers can be cited if they don't keep their vacant lots free of weeds. And despite this association with Christmas, the tumbleweed is still, and most definitely, a weed.

Fortunately, the city owns some undeveloped property where the thistles can mature into a good size without getting ticketed for being unsightly. The land will eventually be used for parks, but the economy has put that sort of development on hold, so the Christmas tree weeds can thrive for the time being. But when lush green spaces replace tumbleweed territory, the crews of weed foragers will have to go forth into the countryside in search of the Yule commodity.

Or they can start importing the weeds from Russia, from whence they originally came.

A Rug for an Extra-Extra-Extra Large Room
Chilchinbito

What may well be the largest Navajo rug ever woven lies rolled up in a local school gymnasium most of the time, but on those occasions when it is opened, it is huge. Larger than huge. Humongous, at the very least.

The rug's dimensions are twenty-eight feet by twenty-four feet, and it took ten Navajo women more than two years to weave the twenty-five tribal designs they incorporated into it. The loom they used, which was set up in the school gym, measured thirty-eight feet long by twenty-five feet tall. When completed in 1979, the rug was displayed at the Navajo Nation Fair in Window Rock, where more than a hundred thousand visitors stopped to examine it. In 1985, it made an appearance at the inauguration of President Ronald Reagan in Washington, DC, and then made stops in Kansas City and Phoenix before it was returned to Chilchinbito, where it was created.

Tribal officials estimate that the cost of the weaving project was about $100,000 in materials and labor, which probably explains why they put a price tag of $5.2 million on it, even though they have no intention of ever selling it.

A small road sign near Chilchinbito proclaims it as the home of the magnificent rug, but now it is unrolled only for school graduation ceremonies. A community of about thirteen hundred, Chilchinbito is located twenty-five miles east of Kayenta on Indian Route 59 on the Navajo Reservation.

Art on the Rocks
Chloride

In these parts, the painted rocks of Chloride are simply known as "the mural." Roy Purcell, the artist, called the work *The Journey* and said it was the result of a deeply personal introspection. Either way, the rock art has withstood the elements, bureaucracy, and those who travel the crooked mile to view it, photograph it, comment on it, and attempt to decipher its hidden meanings.

The mural is both huge and hard to reach. The granite boulders that served as Purcell's canvas rise seventy-five feet above the canyon floor, and some of the painted figures are life-sized times four. The road to the canyon can easily turn the family car into a $750 repair bill, and tour buses can't go there because the trail resembles a path left by a giant serpent with a bad case of hiccups.

Purcell was working as a miner in 1956 when he came across the big rocks and decided to convert them into *objets d'art*. Another miner grubstaked the project by paying for supplies and rounding up some cronies to build scaffolding. Purcell used automobile paint, so the colors are still vibrant.

★ ★

While applying paint to rock one day, Purcell was ordered to stop his work by Bureau of Land Management agents. "I didn't bother to find out who owned the land," he said years later. "So I stopped and ate lunch. They left and I went back to work. They didn't say how long I was supposed to stop. I never heard from them again."

Chloride is about fifteen miles north of Kingman off US Highway 93. The mural is 1.3 miles southeast of the community. To get there, follow the signs on the main street. The road is dirt and difficult, but not impassable. Take your time. Those rocks have been there for millions of years, so they're not going anywhere.

The Keepers of the Croaker
Congress

An old frog squats along State Route 89 about a half mile north of downtown Congress. Although exposed to the Arizona sun almost every day, the creature looks good, perhaps even better than it did when it was born, so to speak, more than three-quarters of a century ago.

But certain features set this amphibian apart. For example, it weighs an estimated sixty tons, stands sixteen feet high, and is made of solid rock. And it needs a face-lift every now and then. The frog, a Congress landmark, existed in its natural state from prehistoric times until 1928, when it underwent a wondrous metamorphosis from rock to art.

Originally, it was just a huge boulder perched on a hillside. Then Sara Perkins, a homesteader's wife, observed that if she squinted her eyes just right, the rock resembled a giant frog. So she and her sons acquired paint, ladders, and brushes and went to work. They painted the boulder green on top and white on the bottom, gave it eyes, spots, and a mouth, and turned it into a tourist attraction. The Perkins family maintained the frog for years, and when they left the area, the citizens of Congress became the unofficial keepers of the croaker.

It's not an easy task because the frog still sits in its original position, so it still requires some ladder-climbing to reach it. One volunteer, Rose

The Congress Frog has withstood the elements
for almost eighty years and gets a new coat
of paint every time it needs one.

Mary Goodson, escaped injury when her ladder slipped while she was
painting. She then became known around town as "the lady who fell
from the frog." Despite that, the giant gets a fresh paint job whenever
the green fades because, as longtime resident George Carter once
observed, "there ain't much else around here to look at so that frog is
important to us."

Mini-Taj in the Desert
Dome

Loren Pratt chuckled when asked if he's ever been compared to Shah Jahan. "No, but it's a nice thought," he said. "I truly loved my wife. This is in her memory."

For those who don't work crossword puzzles and thus don't know about Shah Jahan, he was the Mogul emperor who loved his wife so much that when she died, he had the Taj Mahal built in her memory. It was constructed between 1632 and 1654 near Agra, India, as her mausoleum. Her name was Mumtaz-I-Mahal. Her monument stands nearly 330 feet tall at its highest points, and features a massive double dome sitting atop a 260-foot pinnacle. An estimated seventy thousand men worked on the building.

This tiny shrine near Dome has a close connection to the Taj Mahal in India. Both were built for the love of a woman.

Pratt is a farmer, and his tribute to his late wife, Lois, is not nearly so elegant. It is a tiny wooden chapel that sits on a flat spot in the middle of cotton and lettuce fields. The building stands about fifteen feet tall and can seat six to eight people. With the help of friends and relatives, he constructed it in a few months in 1996. Many of those same people helped with the rebuilding after the chapel suffered severe storm damage in 2011.

The structure is small on the outside and even smaller inside. The pews hold one person comfortably but can accommodate two if they don't mind sitting really close together. "Most visitors come in the winter," Pratt said. "In the summer, they go inside and come out gasping and asking why there's no air-conditioning."

The chapel is located on US Highway 95 about fifteen miles north of Yuma.

The Desert Blooms
Florence

St. Anthony's Greek Orthodox Monastery is an oasis in an otherwise flat piece of desert. In less than twenty years, the monks who live there have built two churches, six chapels, housing, maintenance facilities, rotundas, fountains, and sandstone walkways. They also planted thousands of trees, shrubs, and cactuses, literally converting the once-barren desert into one of the most beautiful spots in Arizona.

Construction began in 1995; the first church was completed within a year. It is one of ten monasteries started in North America by Father Ephraim, a spiritual leader from the Greek Orthodox homeland at Mount Athos in Greece.

Surrounded by foliage and spires, visitors might easily envision themselves in a foreign country. The roofs and columns on the places of worship vary from copper domes to bell towers, and the architecture ranges from brick to stone to lumber.

Visitors are asked to check in at the bookstore directly inside the front gate, where they are welcomed with sweet cakes and pitchers of

The monks who built and reside at St. Anthony's Greek Orthodox Monastery near Florence have turned a piece of desert into a bit of paradise.

ice water. They may then attend services, walk through the grounds, take photographs, and enter the churches.

But there are some restrictions. Men are asked to wear long pants and long-sleeved shirts. Women should wear skirts that hang to the ankles, long-sleeved shirts or blouses, and have their heads covered with a veil or scarf. Hats, caps, sheer scarves, shorts, pant-skirts, mini-skirts, T-shirts, and sleeveless blouses are not allowed. Everyone is asked to wear socks, especially when wearing sandals. A limited supply of temporary proper attire is available at no cost in the bookstore for improperly clad guests. Also, smoking and conversation with the monks are prohibited.

To reach the monastery, take Paisano Road east off State Route 79 about twelve miles south of Florence. Stay on the paved road and it'll lead you directly to the entry.

Lionizing Melvin Jones
Fort Thomas

Distractions are few on this lonely stretch of US Highway 70, where Mount Graham is a bluish-gray mass on the horizon, and a few other peaks rise gently from the flatlands. Otherwise, this two-lane stretch of asphalt zips through cotton fields and small villages without inspiration.

But suddenly, there's this spire standing fifty feet above the semi-desert, standing there all by itself with no church attached. Closer inspection reveals that it's a monument to Melvin Jones. Since a fifty-foot obelisk doesn't just pop out of the ground all by itself, this poses some questions:

Who was Melvin Jones?

And why is his monument way out here next to nowhere?

The answer is obvious to the more than 1.6 million members of Lions International, a worldwide service organization with forty-five thousand clubs around the globe. Melvin Jones, the recognized founder of the Association of Lions Clubs, was born at Fort Thomas on January 13, 1879, the son of a US Cavalry captain and his wife.

The Safford Lions Club financed the monument and dedicated it in 1965. There's also a small Melvin Jones Museum on the site, but it's open only once a year, on the Saturday closest to Jones's January 13 birth date. That's when Lions from all over the world congregate here to roar tribute to their founder.

The monument is on the north side of the highway. Those in need of a lion's share of information should call the Graham County Chamber of Commerce, (888) 837-1841.

A Cornerless House
Gilbert

Don and Carolyn Riedlinger just don't like to see things go to waste. Things like an old barn, an old gristmill, and old granaries. So they recycle them. They turned a barn into a meeting hall. They converted the gristmill into a wedding chapel. And, in their latest move, they reconstructed three old steel granaries into the unusual structure they now call home.

The round granaries had for years served their original purpose as storage units for livestock feed on a nearby dairy farm before the couple acquired them, cut them in half, and moved them onto their property, where they were reassembled as living space. The exterior walls are still the original galvanized metal for the most part, but some of them are now covered with stone facades and vines.

As might be expected, the interiors are round. The walls are insulated and plastered, but it's tough buying circular furniture that matches.

The unique collection had its start in 1994, when the couple bought the 1906 barn in Iowa, dismantled it, and had it shipped piece by piece to Gilbert, where they put it all back together, then sold it to a church. But the church couldn't use it as a congregation hall, so it was returned to the Riedlingers. They took it apart again, and now it sits on their property, awaiting another resurrection.

Three steel granaries were converted into a residence for the Reidlinger family in Gilbert.

Then in 1998, they bought the old Shenandoah Mill in Muddy Creek, Virginia, and utilized three tractor-trailers to haul it back to Gilbert, where they converted it into a popular venue for marriage vows.

To complete their collection, they acquired the granaries in 2006.

The gristmill chapel is at 1359 South Gilbert Road. The triplicate round house is on the south side of Pecos Road between Val Vista Drive and Lindsay Road. And, for the time being, the barn lies in pieces in the backyard.

And Don't Forget Your Helmet
Glendale

Max Beyer's original plan was to hang a few football helmets on the walls to enhance the image of the sports bar he opened in 1979. It was the first establishment of its kind west of the Mississippi River and

★ ★

it needed a theme, so Beyer went with the helmets he'd collected as a hobby.

Typical of such endeavors, it started small, then grew. And grew. And grew. Before his death in the 1990s, Beyer had amassed almost one thousand helmets, far too many for not only his walls but also the display cases he had built. The helmets came from such well-established football institutions as Notre Dame, Michigan, Ohio State, Southern Cal, and Texas, as well as a few lesser-knowns, like Northeast Mississippi, Fayetteville State, Carnegie Mellon, Mankato State, and Coolidge College.

The helmets collected by the late Max Beyer
are still on display in Glendale.

★ ★

One section is devoted to Arizona high school helmets; another is set aside for professional team contributions. Most of them are composed of the tough plastic that is standard for headgear today, but a few are the old leather models, like the one worn by Nusier Salem, who played for Columbus College in 1928.

Beyer also created a fierce-looking creature he called the "Jocko Bird," a hybrid with the head of an eagle and the body of a beer-bellied athlete who wears golf, baseball, football, basketball, hockey, and lacrosse equipment and stands guard at the front door. The establishment, located a 6727 North Forty-Seventh Avenue in Glendale, has changed owners a couple of times since Beyer's death, but it's still known as Max's Sports Bar and Restaurant and, equally important, the helmets and the Jocko Bird are still there.

For directions and menu listings, helmeteers can call (623) 937-1671.

It Sure Looks like a Numbskull
Hillside

Skulls, by their very nature, are usually hidden away where they're hard to find. The Giant Skull of Date Creek is somewhat of an exception. It's right out in the open, and it's been in the exact same spot for more than one hundred years, according to local legend.

The skull is actually a giant boulder painted white with black eyes and a black-rimmed mouth and teeth, so it looks a lot like a real skull even to those who are imaginationally challenged. Like many other pieces of rock art, its origins are hard to trace. But a newspaper clipping in a scrapbook at the Yarnell Public Library sheds some light.

In the clipped-out story, published in the 1960s, former Santa Fe Railroad conductor Lee R. Roberts said he once worked on the passenger trains that roared past the skull. He told the reporter that he would conjure up wild yarns about the discovery of human bones in the area, and then take delight in watching the passengers squirm as the train rounded a bend and the huge skull popped into view.

★ ★

Because of its remote location, this huge rock skull frightens rattlers and other critters but not train passengers.

Roberts said a Santa Fe railroad crew painted the big rock around 1900. They were in charge of painting the mileposts and crossing signs along the tracks, and apparently had some paint and quite a lot of time left over when they finished their assigned task, so they applied both to the boulder. Passenger service is a thing of the past in the area, but the oversize cranium still sits next to the tracks and keeps wide-eyed vigil over the surrounding hills.

Anatomy students and fans of poor Yorick can view the remains by taking Yavapai County Road 62, also known as Date Creek Road, for 6.3 miles west off State Route 89 just north of Congress.

★ ★

A Gathering of Dinosaurs
Holbrook

The real dinosaurs that once roamed the area around Holbrook vanished hundreds of thousands of years ago, but several concrete and bronze replicas have taken up permanent positions in this high desert community.

The most noticeable are the seven giants in a prehistoric pack that welcomes customers to the Indian Rock Shop on the corner of Navajo Boulevard and Joy Nevins Avenue. They range in size from twenty-five

The Lundeen family of Fountain Hills donated their dinosaur to the city of Holbrook.

feet tall to much smaller babies. Adam Luna spent twenty years creating them, using cement, reinforcing rods, and his own hands. On the same side of the street but farther north, a pair of cementosaurs glares at those who pass by Rocks on Route 66, a shop on the corner of California Street and Navajo Boulevard.

In between those two groupings, a more frightening monster leers at tourists and locals alike in the backyard of the Chamber of Commerce office at Navajo Boulevard and Buffalo Drive. It was once part of a group of fourteen dinosaur replicas placed along Interstate 40 near Holbrook as advertising for a nearby museum. When the museum closed, the dinosaurs were sold off. Eight others from that group have found new homes and new tourists to frighten at Jim Gray's Petrified Wood Company, on the intersection of Highways 77 and 18 just south of town.

The lone non-cement member of the herd is a smaller bronze dinosaur that stands in Living West Park on Hopi Drive, just west of the main drag. It was donated to the city by the Lundeen family of Fountain Hills in 1997. The Lundeens bought it in New York, and had it shipped to their home in Fountain Hills where they planned to use it as an outdoor shower next to their swimming pool. But they couldn't find a crane that could lift it over their house, so they gave it to Holbrook.

Always Remember to Shut Your Eyes
Hualapai Indian Reservation

Looking down into the Grand Canyon has always been a test of a person's ability to withstand vertigo. It's thousands of feet from the top to the bottom. And, in most places, the distance is straight down, so most peeks over the edge are of the white-knuckle variety.

And now, in what would seem to be an attempt to make it even scarier, the Hualapai Indians and a Las Vegas developer combined to construct a glass-bottomed walkway that allows those with high queasiness quotients the opportunity to view the canyon while they're jutting out seventy feet into the thin air that surrounds the gorge.

The Skywalk on the Hualapai Indian Reservation lets visitors look almost four thousand feet straight down into the Grand Canyon.

The Grand Canyon Skywalk is part of a forty-million-dollar project designed to turn one thousand acres of reservation land into a tourist attraction. Visitors pay a fee to look down almost four thousand feet into the canyon through the glass bottom and sides of the walkway. It's quite safe. The skywalk is supported by huge steel beams and can accommodate 120 people at once because it was designed to hold seventy-two million pounds, or the equivalent of seventy Boeing 747 jetliners.

It can withstand winds of up to one hundred miles per hour, an earthquake of 8.0 magnitude, and the tremors of 120 uneasy tourists all tightly clutching the guardrails at the same time. Despite that, it's

★ ★

scary, especially when some smart-aleck starts jumping up and down, just to show off.

The attraction is seventy-two miles northeast of Kingman on the Hualapai Reservation. Those who go there might be wise always to keep in mind the cry of the acrophobiac: "Don't look down!"

For more information, call (888) 216-0076 or visit hualapaitours.com.

A Giant Guardian of the Roadway
Kingman

About fifteen miles east of Kingman, at the corner of Route 66 and Anatares Road, a huge green head keeps watchful eyes on the motorists as they pass by. There's something eerie about it, like it popped out of the desert floor after tunneling here from Easter Island, where that famous colony of rock heads resides.

But in reality, it's a work of art called *Giganticus Headicus*, and it was fashioned from wood, metal, and stucco by Gregg Arnold, an artist who moved to the area in 2004 and bought the abandoned RV park where his creation now sits. The concept for the giant head came to him, he told a newspaper reporter, "because the place looked like it needed something like this."

One of the buildings on the site was formerly a bar that was frequented by the likes of actor Jack Klugman, *Star Trek* creator Gene Roddenberry, and, according to legend, Elvis Presley.

But now there's not much there except *Headicus*, a vacant building, some vending machines, and an open invitation to stop and have your photo taken while standing next to a big green tiki-like thing. Despite that, its fame and popularity are growing. Its image was featured in a story about Nissan Infiniti, was the subject of a *Zippy* cartoon strip, and also appears on such promotional items as coffee cups and T-shirts being sold along Route 66.

A giant tiki head watches tourists pass
by on Route 66 near Kingman.

Watching the Bouncing Ball Splatter
Kingman

Sometimes, the ball just doesn't bounce the way it should have. Take, for example, the strange case of Tony Evans, who came to the Arizona desert to test the theory that if a huge ball composed entirely of rubber bands was dropped from a great height, it would bounce high into the sky.

Working at his home in Swansea, Wales, Evans spent five years winding about six million rubber bands into the monster orb. When it

★ ★

was finished, the ball weighed 2,548 pounds and had a circumference of fourteen feet, eight inches, big enough to make it into Guinness World Records. Then an American television program, *Ripley's Believe It Or Not!*, not only offered to sponsor the ball on a tour of the United States, but also to drop it from an airplane to check its bounceability.

The TV crew hauled the sphere to Kingman, where it was loaded onto a plane and flown a mile above the Mohave Desert. As the ball was pushed from the plane, three camera-operating skydivers also leapt into the atmosphere to film the descent, while other cameras recorded the event from the ground. Among the spectators were Evans and his wife, who were flown to the site by the producers of the TV show to watch the big ball bounce.

It didn't happen. The ball hit the desert floor but, instead of bouncing, it shattered apart. The impact created a crater that measured nine feet across and more than three feet deep, and rubber bands were splattered more than two hundred yards away from the landing site.

Despite the failure, Evans wasn't too disappointed. He told reporters covering the event, "To see it come down was fantastic." And he did get a moment of fame when the event appeared on a segment of *Ripley's Believe It Or Not!*

Keeping the Riverbanks Lighted
Lake Havasu City

The rocky shores of New England have lighthouses. So do the coastlines of California, Oregon, and Washington. So do the shorelines of the Great Lakes. And so does Lake Havasu.

This would not be much of an oddity if Lake Havasu wasn't in the middle of the desert. And the lake is a wide spot in a river where nothing larger than a cabin cruiser ever floats by. But there they are, thirteen lighthouses, standing on the banks of the Colorado River as it divides the sandy expanses of the Mohave Desert.

They're not actual lighthouses, like the kind that once warned freighters and ocean liners about the perils of Lake Erie, the rocks off

Miniature lighthouses light the way for sailboats and swimmers at Lake Havasu.

the coast of Maine, and the dangers of the Pacific Ocean along the California coast. The Lake Havasu lighthouses, built and paid for by local residents, are about half-size replicas of the real things, and each one is patterned after an existing structure. The project started in 2002 under the guidance of Bob Keller, a retired real estate agent who constructed one lighthouse all by himself. Each miniature lighthouse has a rotating beacon, and some are used as channel markers to guide the small watercrafts that skim across the waters after dark.

The long-range plan is to erect at least twenty-five lighthouses as a complement to the London Bridge, Lake Havasu City's main tourist attraction. For more information, go to lh-lighthouseclub.org.

Phoenix Is Over Yonder
Mesa

Back when Phoenix was an emerging city with only a minor airport, pilots of small planes coming from the east were often confused about where to find the landing strip. The area was not as developed as it is today, so there was nothing but open desert and plane-gobbling mountains along the eastern border of what is now known as the Valley of the Sun. As a result, some planes flew around in a state of bewilderment while the pilots looked for a place to land.

But then, according to sketchy local lore, either a band of Boy Scouts or flight trainers from nearby Williams Air Field came to the rescue.

More than fifty years ago, Boy Scouts created a sign to guide pilots to the airport in Phoenix.

In the 1950s, one story goes, as part of an Eagle Scout project, a group of scouts cleared away brush and rocks on a southern slope of the Usery Mountains. Then they whitewashed a whole bunch of the rocks and used them to form a huge PHOENIX fronted by a large arrow on the mountainside. The arrow pointed west, toward the airport almost thirty miles away, and the sign supposedly served its purpose of aiming pilots in the right direction for several years. But others claim flight instructors from Williams Field placed it there in the 1930s so their trainees could find their way to the Phoenix landing area.

Regardless of which group was responsible, the Valley of the Sun has grown so much that houses are closing in on the sign, and US Highway 60 below aims directly at the airport so its usefulness has ended. Its location, however, is still known as Signal Butte.

The sign remains in pretty good shape, considering that it has been there for more than fifty years. Another group of scouts repainted it in the 1990s, but that will probably be the last upgrade. Homeowners and conservationists have protested that the big word is way too much verbiage that creates an eyesore in the natural beauty.

The Return of the Diving Lady

Mesa

For more than a half-century, the Diving Lady was a splashy neon icon along US Highway 60. But her aquatic days appeared to be over when a windstorm put an end to her three-stage dives. Fortunately for lovers of kitsch and nostalgia, she's back.

She beckoned those travelers who passed by the Starlite Motel for decades, skillfully performing her neon-lit springboard plunge into a blue neon pool in endless succession. But a storm on October 5, 2010, put a temporary end to her lengthy career. The wind toppled the seventy-eight-foot pole that supported the lady, so her last dive was to the unyielding pavement of the motel parking lot. The impact shattered all the neon tubing and twisted the metal that held it. The work of designer Stanley Russon and signmaker Paul Millet lay as a battered heap, apparently beyond repair.

But news of her ill fortune spurred a recovery effort. Within weeks, the Mesa Preservation Foundation began raising the estimated one hundred thousand dollars needed to put her back on the springboard. The group paired with Larry Graham, a Millet protégé, and the reconstruction began. The neon figures were put on display in shopping malls as workers refinished the six-and-a-half-foot M, O, T, E, L letters that hang opposite the diver on the new pole.

The lady (or three ladies) was put back in her original spot in January 2013, so now she dives nightly and endlessly once again.

The Starlite Motel is at 2710 E. Main. Call (480) 964-2201.

Burros and Biscuits
Oatman

The unofficial census rolls for Oatman contain twelve to fourteen burros and 150 humans. The burros are listed first because they provide much of the economic base for the humans.

The animals are descendants of the working burros that were turned loose in the desert by miners more than a century ago. They come down from the surrounding hills every day and take up their posts along Oatman's main drag. There they consort with the tourists, many of whom come here especially to go one-on-one with a burro. And the tourists feed the burros, take pictures of burros, and buy burro postcards.

Most merchants, therefore, offer a wide variety of burro-related items, including burro feed, burro figurines made of papier-mâché and goat hair, burro T-shirts, burro bumper stickers, and burro calendars. The bumper stickers and calendars are big sellers. Because the burro is also known as an ass, those items substitute "burro" for "ass" anytime they can, as in "hauling burro" and "kicking some burro."

The animals have the run of the city during their daily forays, and motorists are cautioned that hitting a burro will result in a major fine.

★ ★

During the foaling season, the person who first spots a newborn hangs a notice on the city bulletin board in the post office, and the town gives it a name.

And, of course, the burros also provide the essential equipment for the annual Burro Biscuit Toss. Prior to the event, volunteers go forth into the desert to select used burro feed that has been recycled

**Burros are a major economic force in Oatman,
so they can go where they please.**

through the burros into burro droppings. Desert droppings are pre-
ferred to those left on Main Street because they're harder and hold
their shape better when propelled. The biscuits are painted gold, and
contestants pick their favorites and toss them down the street in front
of crowds of cheering spectators. The biscuit that soars the farthest is
declared the winner. The tossing champion gets cash and merchandise
prizes, as well as a fresh bar of soap.

The event is held during Gold Camp Days over the Labor Day weekend. Biscuiteers needing more information should call (928) 768-6222
or visit oatmangoldroad.com.

The Curse of the Rocks
Petrified Forest National Park

Signs throughout the Petrified Forest National Park warn visitors not to
remove pieces of petrified wood, not even the tiny little ones just lying
there on the ground. There are fines for such acts, and the fines are
stiff—up to $275 for taking just a sliver.

But even worse is "the Curse."

An exhibit at the Rainbow Forest Museum, which serves as a visitor center at the south end of the park, is filled with testimonials from
petty thieves, rock hounds, and others who made off with some of the
pieces. Many of the letters from repentant visitors deal with the problems that followed the crimes.

"I am returning the rock and the bad luck that followed it," wrote
one penitent. "Since I have had it, my bike has been stolen and my
feet had blisters as big as my hand. And I know my side hurts and it
might be a hurnea [sic] and worse [sic] of all me and my girlfriend are
about to brake [sic] up . . . "

Another tortured soul confessed, "[We] smuggled out three small
pieces of petrified wood, carefully stuck inside a bra on the body. That
evening our bad luck began. One person had stomach cramps and
diarrhea. . . . That same night we were the only ones to be attacked
by flying ants in the campground."

Park rangers say they receive two or three packages containing misappropriated petrified wood every week. Sometimes the returned rocks come from family members ashamed of what their kinfolk did. Like this one:

"I don't know what possessed my father to take a piece of wood. . . . To this day I remember him placing it in a pack of cigarettes. . . . It was a part of my rock collection as a child but even then I knew it was wrong."

But for many others, the price is higher than guilt. Here's an example:

"Not known to me, my husband took several fossils from the park. Bad luck has plagued us ever since. His mother and my mother died, and my cousin, who was also my best friend, died. My husband had an affair. . . . Later, he lost his job and we became financially strapped . . . and *[he]* became a hard-drinking stranger. Please accept these cursed fossils with my blessing."

The Petrified Forest National Park is off Interstate 40 east of Holbrook. For details on the curse and other matters, call (928) 524-6228 or visit nps.gov/pefo/index.htm. And if you go there, remember to take only pictures, not rocks.

Look! Up in the Sky! It's a . . . Mushroom?
Phoenix

One of the recent additions to the city's array of public art is quite large and somewhat difficult to figure out. Since being installed in the Phoenix Civic Space Park in 2009, the work has drawn substantial comment. Not all of it has been favorable.

The artist, Janet Echelman, calls it *Her Secret Is Patience*, a phrase taken from an essay by Ralph Waldo Emerson that reads: "Leave this military hurry and adapt the pace of nature. Her secret is patience." Echelman said the project was designed to emulate the patterns of desert winds; critics say it looks like an enormous mushroom. Or a miniature tornado. Or a wormhole. One reviewer referred to it as "a

Wire, imagination, and air are the major components of a large work of art in downtown Phoenix.

drab, heavy fisherman's net." Since it cost about $2.4 million to create and install, others have called it "a total waste of taxpayer money."

Despite that, it is impressive. And curious. So curious that it grows on you. It's a huge netlike creation that hangs from two rings suspended between three poles that stand from 105 to 145 feet tall. The rings measure thirty feet in diameter, and the lowest part of the work is thirty-eight feet above the ground. The nets are composed of galvanized steel cables and polyester braided twine netting, so the piece changes shape with the slightest breeze but is built to withstand Arizona's fierce winds that accompany the usual thunderstorms and monsoons. When the sun is shining, the sculpture casts patterned shadows; at night, the built-in illumination gradually changes its coloration.

The "secret" art has already endeared itself to most of those who take a close look. It's located in a small park on First Avenue just south of Fillmore Avenue in downtown Phoenix.

'Rithmetic in the Round
Phoenix

The Robert L. Duffy High School takes academic architecture all the way to the outer limits of our universe. The campus, located at 2550 E. Jefferson Street near downtown Phoenix, is small but eye-catching because all four buildings are large monolithic structures with domes painted to look like the planets Earth, Neptune, Saturn, and Jupiter.

Despite their unusual exteriors, all four function as regular class-rooms. Earth houses a one-hundred-seat gymnasium, full basketball court, and an elevated two-lane track (it takes twenty-three round trips to equal one mile). Some students use the latest technology to learn about computers and astronomy in Jupiter; others take acting classes and present plays in the 120-seat interior of the Neptune dome. And young mothers can leave their children in the day care center inside Saturn, where they also take child development classes.

Each building is totally solar-powered and equipped with the latest technology. Also, the twenty-five-thousand-square-foot parking lot is covered with a solar-reflective green substance that reduces summer surface heat by as much as thirty degrees.

The school, which offers both core curriculum and career-focused classes, was erected in 2010 and has room for 240 students. And, of course, the student teams are nicknamed the Comets.

★ ★

Students at Robert L. Duffy High School attend classes in planet-shaped buildings.

For directions on how to view the universe without leaving the confines of Earth, go to careersuccessschools.com and click on the link to Robert L. Duffy High School.

A Signed Centennial Sign
Phoenix

If you drive by the old warehouse on the northeast corner of Seventh Street and Lincoln Avenue in downtown Phoenix, it's very possible that you'll think it's a hasty repair job thrown onto the east side of the structure. The entire eastern side is covered with highway signs, like DO

★ ★

NOT PASS, REDUCED SPEED AHEAD, and KEEP RIGHT EXCEPT TO PASS. Some have no words, just recognizable symbols like a twisty arrow that warns of an oncoming serpentine stretch of road, a red octagon that tells you there's a stop sign ahead, and a black P surrounded by a red circle with a slash through it, indicating no parking.

Used street signs denote Arizona's centennial celebration in downtown Phoenix.
LYN LOWE

★ ★

There are more than five hundred of them, but they're art, not a bad repair job. Michael Levine, a Phoenix real estate developer, had them attached to the building in honor of Arizona's centennial celebration. Those who take the time to look will notice that integrated into the signs are the numbers 1912 and 2012, denoting Arizona's one hundred years of statehood.

Levine purchased the signs from an Arizona state surplus yard more than a decade ago and used them to promote Levine's Machines, his agency that specializes in buying and restoring old abandoned warehouses. But in 2011, he decided to put the YIELD, NO LEFT TURN, and LITTERING HIGHWAYS UNLAWFUL signage to centennial use. He used a computer to lay out the design and make some necessary adjustments. Then crews using scissor hoists and battery-powered screwdrivers worked for more than six days and used three thousand self-drilling screws to affix the signs to the warehouse.

And those who stop and study the tin mural might find some of the messages Levine hid in the project. "It's a graphic design," he said. "The speed signs, for example, are arranged to reflect how we have developed over the past century."

The signed building contains about ten thousand square feet of space, and it's for lease. For information, call (602) 510-1455.

A Multitude of Mini-Machines
Prescott

Some things were meant to be together: peanut butter and jelly, fish and chips, french fries and ketchup, the John W. Kalusa Miniature Aircraft Collection and Embry-Riddle Aeronautical University.

Especially the John W. Kalusa Miniature Aircraft Collection and Embry-Riddle Aeronautical University.

The collection consists of 5,829 miniature flying machines, each painstakingly carved over a half-century by John W. Kalusa of Mesa. Using only balsa wood and a razor blade, he crafted every model to an exact scale of one-eighteenth of an inch to one foot. The consistent

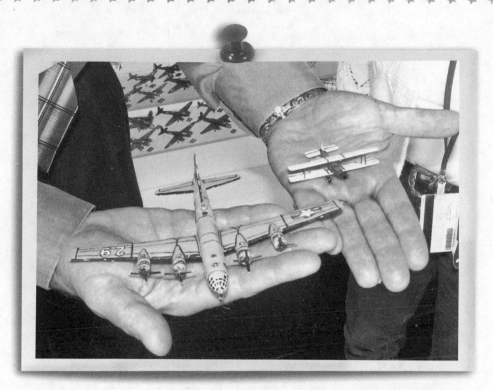

**The Kalusa Miniature Aircraft Collection is on display at
Embry-Riddle Aeronautical University in Prescott.**

use of the scale gave every one of his models an accurate size relation-
ship to the others.

After Kalusa's death in 2003, his family donated the mini-planes
to the aviation and aerospace university, which put them on display
in its new library. Each model is delicately painted, right down to the
detailed markings characteristic of the actual aircraft. This required a
steady hand because many of the planes have wingspans of less than
two inches.

Kalusa began this avocation in 1936 at the age of fourteen, when he
made World War I models for a battle game. After serving in World War
II, he started up again, creating all sorts of aircraft, from bombers to hot
air balloons, from rockets to helicopters, from biplanes to jet fighters.

His goal was to make a tiny replica of every private, commercial, military, and rocket aircraft ever built. He also drew detailed specification sheets for each model, giving the full-size dimensions of the originals.

In 2003, his work was selected as the largest collection of hand-made airplanes in the world by Guinness World Records. Mini-pilots and others may view the collection during library hours. The university is located at 3700 Willow Creek Road. For more information, visit library.pr.erau.edu/collections/kalusa.php or call (928) 777-3758.

In Memory of Mike
Prescott

The Courthouse Plaza, downtown Prescott's centerpiece, is a square block that encompasses a stately old courthouse, a large gazebo, statues of heroes, benches, a time map, and a small plaque that honors the memory of a stray dog.

The dog's name was Mike, but most people called him "the community mutt." His territory was Whiskey Row—an entire block once filled with taverns, bars, saloons, and other forms of spirits dispensaries—and Mike regarded it as his own. He made daily rounds, kept other dogs away, and was rewarded with never-ending handouts from bar owners and patrons.

In 1957, a local judge decreed that Mike was an outlaw because he wasn't licensed. This created a minor dilemma because Mike was a town pet and didn't belong to anybody. It was resolved when several Prescott policemen raised enough money to pay for the tags and shots.

After Mike died in 1960, the *Prescott Courier* ran his obituary on the front page, and a letter to the editor suggested a permanent memorial in his honor because of his friendly attitude and high regard for his fellow citizens. The plaque, paid for by the people he had befriended during his fifteen-year reign along Whiskey Row, was placed in the northwest corner of the plaza where it remains. It reads, in part, "He was a silent, loyal, tolerant friend. Take heed if you will, a moral lies herein."

★ ★

He Never Worries about Having "Nothing to Wear"
Quartzsite

Paul Winer gets up every morning, dresses, and goes to work. Getting dressed doesn't take long because he basically wears the same thing every day—a cowboy hat, sunglasses, sandals, and a necklace. That's all. Except for the leather thong that covers a small area located at the confluence of his left thigh and his right thigh.

Once attired, Winer heads to Reader's Oasis Books, his place of business, where signs at the front door inform potential customers

**Naturist Paul Winer sells his personalized
bookmarks at his Quartzsite bookstore.**

that the owner is friendly, but he's not wearing much clothing. Winer greets those who enter with a smile and solid handshake, and then identifies himself as a naturalist, not a nudist. He's pretty casual about the sparse nature of his clothing, probably because he's been dressing that way ever since childhood. If they ask, he'll tell his customers about his early life, when he performed as a next-to-naked musician known as Sweet Pie. He played up and down the East Coast, he says, and also spent a lot of time in court defending his choice (or lack) of attire.

Shortly after Winer moved to Quartzsite and opened his bookstore, local officials tried to pass an ordinance against his lifestyle, but it fizzled. Now he's a town icon who tends to his massive collection of books, magazines, compact discs, and periodicals, most of them used, all of them arranged on shelves that take up almost every inch of indoor space.

Many who frequent his establishment are winter visitors who already know about his wardrobe, and probably would never be seen in a place like this when they're back home. Several of them buy something; several more ask him to pose for photographs, and he willingly agrees. If they don't have a camera, they can buy a bookmark that bears a full-body color photo of Winer giving a thumbs-up sign while attired in his regular attire. Or lack thereof.

Winer does make one occasional departure from his way of life. In winter, he dons a sweater. But it only goes to his waist.

The bookstore is located at 690 East Main Street.

It's a Rye Humor
Rye

When he was still in business, Ron Adler said he liked to make people smile. But sometimes when they visited All Bikes, his two-acre lot filled with old frames and wheels, they'd break down in tears. "There's just something about seeing your first bike again," he'd explain. "A bike is your first sense of freedom. You're not with your mom and dad anymore. You're on your own."

Ron Adler deals in memories and old
bicycles on his acreage near Rye.

★ ★

For years, Adler's collection of Monarchs, Schwinns, Whizzers, and Black Phantoms marched across his hillside property like an army of circular steel and chrome. From the road, they looked like they'd been dumped there and left to rot, but there was actually some organization among the rows. Only Adler himself, however, knew where everything was.

Back then, he claimed he had no idea how many old bikes languished under his care. "If you really have to know," he'd tell those who asked, "you'll have to count them yourself." The offer was never accepted, but any quick estimate would have put the number in the thousands. Adler began his operation in the Pacific Northwest, then moved it to Rye in 1988. He sold parts and entire two-wheelers to customers all over the world.

But it all ended early in the summer of 2013, when a quick-moving forest fire destroyed not only his enterprise, but several other businesses in Rye, a small hamlet located on State Route 87. Some of them may return, but Adler has no plans to start over again.

The Fighting Artichokes

Salt River–Pima Maricopa Indian Community

The Scottsdale Community College athletic teams are nicknamed the Artichokes. It's a classic case of turning a lemon into lemonade. Or, in this case, an artichoke into art.

This journey into the world of jockstrap-wearing vegetables began during the school's formative years in the early 1970s. A dispute arose between students and the administration about which function should be the most important—athletics or academics. The administration wanted to emphasize athletics to attract media attention and income. The students envisioned more money for classrooms, scholarships, and learning.

The college constitution gave students a voice in budget matters, but when the school built a $1.7 million gymnasium without their approval, the Artichoke Movement formed. In an apparent

Former Scottsdale Community College
student Michel Leckband as the school's
mascot, the Fighting Artichoke
SCOTTSDALE COMMUNITY COLLEGE

★ ★

peacemaking attempt, the administration asked the student government to hold an election to select a mascot. Instead, the offer infuriated the student senators, who retaliated by selecting three rather dubious mascot choices: the Artichoke, the Rutabaga, or the Scoundrel. The Artichoke won, but the administration declared the election invalid.

After months of bickering, another election officially approved the Artichoke, and also picked pink and green as school colors. The administration balked at pink-clad athletes, however, so both sides agreed on a compromise. The mascot name would stay, but the teams would become the blue-and-white clad Artichokes, hardly a fashion statement. Eventually, the college adopted a more appropriate green and gold color scheme.

Ironically, the episode produced what school officials were looking for: publicity. The name attracted international attention and is still a frequent subject for both electronic and print media. And in 2002, the institution introduced a line of Artie Artichoke dolls as a marketing gimmick.

At first, the institution also had a mascot who showed up at football games wearing a homemade artichoke costume. School lore says he was dismissed because he never washed his uniform and, as most gourmets know, there's nothing worse than an overripe artichoke. The wife of a faculty member created a new costume that is still in use.

Vegetarians and jocks can find more information at scottsdalecc .edu. The school is located at 9000 East Chaparral Road on the Salt River-Pima Maricopa Indian Community along the Loop 101 Expressway.

A Sailing Ship of the Desert?
Scottsdale

So you're driving along near the corner of Scottsdale and McDowell Roads and, suddenly, up pops this thing that looks like an oversize sailing vessel. A huge ship. A ship so big that it could hold the *Nina, Pinta,* and *Santa Maria* and still have room for several yachts. Or, depending upon your imagination, maybe it looks like a big circus tent. An exceptionally big circus tent. A circus tent so big it could hold a dozen circuses with a full complement of trained elephants.

But it's actually SkySong, more properly known as Arizona State University's Innovation Center, a mixed-use project that will eventually consist of 1.2 million square feet of office, research, and retail space, plus a hotel and conference center.

The big sail-looking sheets are the project's focal point. They rise 125 feet above the surrounding buildings and contain 50,000 square feet of Teflon-coated fiberglass material.

The architects designed them to shade those who work in the facility, as well as those who visit for business reasons, out of curiosity, or to shop at the outdoor markets that occasionally set up beneath them.

Billowing sails in the desert denote the SkySong complex in Scottsdale.

★ ★

The faux sails were built to withstand every type of weather, including high winds and summer thunderstorms. But they didn't have to worry about snow, this being the Sonoran Desert where the average snowfall measures in millimeters. Or less.

What's a Good Name? Ask Nola
Sierra Vista

Back in 1954, the community now known as Sierra Vista was little more than low-income housing that surrounded and served nearby Fort Huachuca. Although there wasn't much there, the residents decided to incorporate, so a group formed, met, and set the wheels in motion. They took out petitions, got the necessary signatures, and asked the state legislature for approval.

One of the required steps was selecting a town name. They area had previously been known as both Fry and Carmichael, but few wanted either of those, so the committee asked the citizenry to sub-mit more appropriate suggestions. The most submitted name would be declared the winner. Included on the list were Buena, Garden City, and Nola Walker's favorite: Sierra Vista. Walker was a thirty-three-year-old housewife at the time, and she said the name came to her as she looked at the Huachuca Mountains to the south.

Because there were no city offices, the woman who served as community clerk had to use the trunk of her car to store the ballots. Worried that they might get lost, she asked Nola Walker to keep them.

A while later, a man representing the soon-to-be-city called Mrs. Walker from Phoenix and said the incorporation had been approved. But, he added, they needed the new name right away. Without hesi-tation, she replied, "It's Sierra Vista." Assuming that Sierra Vista had been the popular choice, the officials in charge dutifully applied it to the new city.

Years later, however, Mrs. Walker revealed what had actually hap-pened. "I put those cards [ballots] into a drawer and forgot all about them," she said in 2006, while recalling the incident during the city's fiftieth anniversary celebration. "When they told me they needed the name right away, I said it was Sierra Vista. Then I took all those cards and threw them in the trash. I never even looked at them."

So even today, nobody knows for sure which name actually won the contest. But the residents have forgiven, and even thanked, Mrs. Walker. She was awarded a Certificate of Forgiveness during the 2006 festivities, and also rode on a parade float declaring her "the Woman Who Named Sierra Vista."

A Really Full House
Snowflake

This a two-house story, as opposed to a two-story house.

Back in 1878, Andrew Rogers and his family migrated to what was then a very small community in northeastern Arizona, where Rogers built a one-room cabin. As his family grew, Rogers added more rooms to the modest structure. In fact, he added so many rooms that the new construction eventually swallowed up the original building. And over the years, as the home site passed from family to family, all memory and mention of the log cabin disappeared.

It stayed that way until 1989, when the house of many add-ons caught fire. While cleaning the debris after the flames were extinguished, workmen found the little cabin standing amid the ashes. The thick logs had withstood the blaze, probably because all the additions had protected them.

The city of Snowflake recognized the cabin as a valuable piece of the town's history and moved it to a new location at First West and Center Streets. Volunteers gave it a new roof and porch, then stocked it with period furniture, including a bearskin spread that covers a rope bed.

The cabin is now open to the public. Visit snowflaketaylor chamber .org.

★ ★

When an old house burned in Snowflake, firemen found an original log cabin in the ashes.

The Mysterious Juniper
Sunset Point

Every year around Thanksgiving, just north of the rest stop known as Sunset Point, travelers along Interstate 17 between Phoenix and Flagstaff start looking for "the juniper." Most of the time, it's just a sort of scraggly bush-like tree, similar to the thousands of others that line the road. But when the holiday season arrives, this particular juniper blossoms.

Not in the botanical sense, however.

For more than three decades, parties unknown have toiled in the darkness to adorn the tree with Christmas decorations—tinsel, ornaments, and ribbons. So now, whenever the Yuletide approaches, the "Mystery Christmas Tree" delights motorists as they near Milepost 254. And then, there it is—sparkling and shining in the high desert sunlight.

There are countless rumors about who's responsible. Speculation ranges from Santa's elves to State Highway Patrolmen to Department of Transportation workers. Journalists have tried to dig out the story behind it all, but have not been successful. And when the tree was imperiled by a range fire a few years ago, firefighters on the scene

Phantom adorners decorate a lonesome juniper bush prior to most holidays.
LYN LOWE

★ ★

credited "a higher power" for saving it. Others claim they know who does the desert decor, but refuse to name names because it would ruin the magic.

So the legend continues. And grows. Recently, it has been adorned with red, white, and blue ribbons to denote Independence Day, and yellow ribbons to honor overseas servicemen.

No Help for *The Helping Hand*
Superior

The town square here isn't very big. In fact, it's more of a triangle than a square, and a small one at that. So small that if it weren't for the statue, there's a good chance that nobody would notice it. But the statue gives it purpose.

It's called *The Helping Hand*, and it depicts a man reaching down to help a friend. It was hewn from a fifteen-ton chunk of dacite by a reluctant sculptor named Tom Macias.

It was a spur-of-the-moment situation, Macias says now. Back in 1982, the Superior Beautification Committee was tossing around ideas for the community's centennial celebration. "A friend volunteered me," Macias claims. "He says, 'Tom, why don't you do a sculpture?' And before I could refuse, I was involved."

Macias had taken a couple of college art classes but had no formal training as a sculptor. There was also the problem of finding the right rock. If it was big enough, Macias couldn't handle it. If it wasn't big enough, it wouldn't be impressive. A geologist solved the problem when he found one that would work, and the Kennicott mining company sent a flatbed truck after it, then delivered it to Macias. "A bunch of guys came over that night and kind of horsed around," Macias says. "We all had our pictures taken, holding hammers and wearing hard hats. But then they all left and I was all by myself with a fifteen-ton rock and virtually no tools."

The rock was lying flat so Macias had to get a front-end loader to stand it up. His tool inventory consisted of a small hammer and a couple of chisels. And the dedication ceremony was only seventy-five days away. Little by little, the novice sculptor acquired the necessary equipment and skills to complete the project, but it was close. At midnight on the eve of the dedication, Macias was still putting on—or, rather, taking off—the finishing touches.

Macias is still a part-time artist, but he hasn't tried anything monumental since. The sculpture sits on the town's main street, just north of US Highway 60.

The Multi-Blasted Anvil
Taylor

The people who reside in this northeastern Arizona community don't need an alarm clock to wake them early so they don't miss the Fourth of July festivities. The Taylor Fire Department makes certain they don't oversleep.

And they do it with a bang.

A rather loud bang.

Starting at 4 a.m. every July 4, the department conducts an annual ritual known as "firing the anvil." It's a simple procedure: Get a sixty-pound anvil and some gunpowder, stuff a batch of gunpowder under the anvil, light the fuse, and stand back. (The warning of "Do not try this at home" should be rather obvious here.)

Once the glowing fuse reaches the gunpowder, the ensuing blast not only wakes up everyone within hearing distance, it also catapults the anvil several feet into the air. Then it falls back to the ground with a resounding *clank!*

The firemen repeat the process until everyone in Taylor is awake and ready to celebrate. And no anvils are hurt during the process.

Residents of Taylor get an early Fourth of July
wake-up call during the firing of the anvil.

The Day the Big Bubble Burst
Tempe

Ordinarily, when a dam breaks, the incident is accompanied by
crashes, bangs, thunderous roars, and other sounds of catastrophe.
But the dam holding back Tempe Town lake is not ordinary, so when
it broke, it didn't go *bang* or *crash* or *boom*. It merely went *pop*.

The lake is a man-made impoundment of the Salt River. It's two
miles long, eight hundred to twelve hundred feet wide and seven to
nineteen feet deep. By using a rather complicated formula, officials

have determined that the lake contains 977 million gallons of water. The only things holding back all that liquid is a series of inner tubes.

They are not, however, the type of inner tubes found in a bicycle repair shop. Instead, each is an inch-thick rubber fabric bladder that measures 225 feet in length and weighs forty tons. The sections are bolted to concrete slabs at both ends of the lake. On the night of July 20, 2010, one of the bladders on the west end of the lake went *pop!* and broke apart. Within seconds, almost a billion gallons of water had escaped into the normally dry Salt River bed.

Since the lake is an economic boon to the city, restoration began a short time later. By late October, all the bladders and all the water had been replaced, new fish hatchlings were released, and the boaters and anglers lived happily ever after.

At least, for the time being.

To prevent a similar occurrence, Tempe officials are now considering a very expensive permanent dam composed of concrete and steel.

The Incredible, Inedible Cake Buildings
Tempe and Phoenix

Most buildings look like buildings, but there are deviations. In the Valley of the Sun, for example, a church meeting hall resembles a flying saucer and a governmental building is an upside down pyramid. But among the favorites for sheer quirkiness is a trio that conjures up visions of happy songs, candles, and best wishes. Two of them are on the Arizona State University campus; the third is nearby in Phoenix.

ASU's Grady Gammage Auditorium is the best known and architecturally outstanding. It was designed by famed architect Frank Lloyd Wright and was originally scheduled to be constructed in Baghdad, Iraq. But the building was never erected in the Middle East and the plans were shelved until 1957, when then-ASU president Grady Gammage contacted Wright about designing a concert hall.

Wright produced his old plans, the deal was made, and construction began in 1962. Neither Gammage nor Wright lived to see the

Grady Gammage Auditorium on the Arizona State University campus was designed by Frank Lloyd Wright.

The Music Hall at Arizona State University looks like a giant birthday cake.

The Tovrea Castle resembles a
three-tiered wedding cake.

completion. The first event staged in the $2.46 million venue was
a performance by the Philadelphia Orchestra, conducted by Eugene
Ormandy, on September 18, 1964. The interior of the auditorium contains three thousand seats, all of them within 115 feet of the stage.
The circular exterior is adorned with columns and scallops, giving it a
definite appearance of an extravagant wedding cake.

Not more than one hundred yards away, the ASU Music Building
sort of mirrors the Gammage Auditorium with its round shape, massive
size, and swooping architectural loops. Built in 1970, it was designed

★ ★

by Wesley Peters, who was Wright's son-in-law. Music students who attend classes inside refer to it as "the birthday cake building."

It also houses a music theater, music library museum, music research facility, concert hall, recital halls, and a hand-carved eighteen-hundred-pipe organ.

Both structures are visible on Mill Avenue as it turns into Apache Boulevard adjacent to the campus.

About a mile from ASU, the Tovrea Castle sits atop a cactus-studded hill. When he erected the building in 1928, Alessio Carraro intended it to be a resort hotel. Working without blueprints, Carraro created a structure in the form of four elongated octagons sitting on each other, and then topped it with a windowed tower. The end result was a building that looks more like a multi-tiered cake than a hotel.

He called it Carraro Heights, but his dream vanished when the Tovrea family installed a meat packing plant and feeder lot right next to his property, He eventually sold out to the Tovreas, who moved into the building and stayed there until 1969.

The City of Phoenix bought the castle in the 1990s and, by 2012, had converted it into a tourist attraction and reception venue open to the public. It's on Van Buren Street between 48th and 52nd Streets.

The Poker Game That Went On . . . And On . . . And On . . .
Tombstone

The Bird Cage Theatre was built to be an opera house, which prob-ably explains why it was originally called the Elite. But it didn't serve in that capacity very long. A short time after it opened, it was renamed the Bird Cage Theatre and was soon known across the nation a "the toughest, bawdiest and most wicked nightspot between Basin Street and the Barbary Coast," as an 1884 issue of the *New York Times* described it.

Instead of becoming a venue for sopranos and tenors singing arias from *Rigoletto* and *Aida*, the building became a combination saloon, gambling hall, and house of ill repute. For nine consecutive years, the

★ ★

The Bird Cage Theatre in Tombstone served as an opera house, brothel, and site of a never-ending poker game.

place never shut its doors, and the second-story boxes designed to give opera buffs a good view of the stage were converted into cribs where the ladies of the evening plied their trade. During that time, local historians have found, there is evidence of sixteen gun and knife fights that resulted in twenty-six deaths, and the ceilings, walls, and floors are still peppered by forty visible bullet holes.

The lower level, which was opened to the public in 2002, once hosted a poker game that went on uninterrupted twenty-four hours a day for eight years, five months, and three days. The buy-in was one thousand dollars, and an estimated one million dollars changed hands during the span. Among those who sat in were Doc Holliday, George Randolph Hearst, Diamond Jim Brady, and Bat Masterson. And while all that was going on, Wyatt Earp and Josephine Marcus were carrying on their illicit love affair in a nearby room.

The theater/brothel/saloon, located at the east end of Allen Street, is now a major tourist attraction in Tombstone, open daily except Christmas. For more information, call (520) 457-3421 or visit tombstone birdcage.com.

Rattlin' over Broadway
Tucson

The Diamondback Bridge can probably lay claim to several titles, like "the world's largest rattlesnake," "the world's longest rattlesnake," and even "the world's most artistic use of steel floor grating."

The pedestrian bridge—three hundred feet long, sixteen feet high, and sixteen feet across—spans Broadway, a major traffic artery. It's the creation of Tucson artist Simon Donovan, who observed, "the proportions of the bridge seemed to be perfect for depicting a large snake." And so he made one.

Donovan selected steel floor grating and had it rolled into a vaulted form to make the snake's body. When it came time to paint it, he created giant templates from huge sheets of rubber koi pond liner and attached them to the form with masking tape. "It looked like Lilliputians tying Gulliver down," he said.

Pedestrians can enter through either end. The mouth is fully agape and supported by two iron beams that look suspiciously like fangs. At the other end there's a giant rattle pointing skyward, and an electronic eye catches the movement of pedestrians and sets off the eerie sound of a rattler's warning.

The snake's mouth is on Iron Horse Park at First Avenue and Tenth Street. Don't be afraid to use it. But on the other hand, it's probably not a good idea to go through it while singing, "Fangs for the Memories."

What's the better choice—walking through the belly of a snake or walking across rush-hour traffic? Tucson pedestrians get to choose daily.

A Holy Treasure?

Tumacacori National Monument

According to those who spend a considerable portion of their lives searching for the alleged treasures buried across Arizona, there's a fortune hidden beneath the floor of Tumacacori National Monument, the old mission south of Tubac.

The legends say that the church was once not only a place of worship but also a mill and smelter for a gold and silver mining operation run by Jesuit missionaries in the first half of the nineteenth century.

There are two legendary scenarios. In one, the missionaries learned they were being called back to Spain so they loaded nearly three thousand burros with precious metal, carried the treasure to the mine, then sealed and buried the entrance in the hope that they'd be able to come back and retrieve it. But they were never allowed to leave Spain, so now an estimated twenty-five million dollars in gold and silver may lie under the sacred ground.

In the second version, the missionaries found a rich silver mine nearby and forced the Opata Indians to work for them. After the ore was smelted into bars, it was stored in a huge room under the mission. The Indians also used the room for religious ceremonies, which were a combination of their own pagan beliefs and the missionaries' preaching. At one point, the legends claim, they sacrificed a young maiden to their gods when she refused to marry a chieftain and bear him a son, who they believed would be a savior. When the priests found out, they drove the Indians away, and then sealed the mine without recovering the wealth.

Or so the stories go.

But don't go rushing off to Tumacacori with pick and shovel in the hope of getting rich. The old mission is now a national monument, so digging holes is not only severely frowned upon, it's also strictly forbidden.

Why Why Is Why
Why

Many years ago, perhaps even longer ago than that, Peggy and Jim Kater settled down on a piece of land near the Little Ajo Mountains, just a little bit north of the Mexican border. Because their homestead was near the junction of State Routes 85 and 86, and because the junction formed a Y-intersection, they simply called it "the Y."

Eventually, the area surrounding the Y attracted enough others so that the community needed a post office. And when the Postmaster General requested a town name, the Katers said it should be Y, like it always had been. But Arizona law required that all city names must have at least three letters, so the named was changed to Why because (a) people were always asking why anybody would live in such a remote place, and (b) because "Why" rhymes with "Y."

The Arizona Department of Transportation later removed the old Y-intersection for safety reasons and replaced it with a conventional T-intersection. But Why is still Why, and most everyone who goes there still asks why.

Finally, a Corner for Standin' On
Winslow

For a long time, people would come to Winslow just to stand on a corner. The problem was, they were never sure which corner to stand on. But thanks to some farsighted people who know how corner-standers like to have a place of their own, the dilemma has been resolved. Now there is an official Standin' On the Corner in Winslow Arizona Park in Winslow, Arizona.

This came about because of a line in the song "Take It Easy," written by Jackson Browne and Glenn Frey and recorded by the Eagles in 1972. It became the group's signature song, and is one of the Rock and Roll Hall of Fame's "500 songs that shaped rock and roll." The line refers to a young man who was "standin' on a corner" in Winslow when a girl in a flatbed truck slows down to check him out.

As parks go, this one isn't much, size-wise. It's only 30 feet wide and 134 feet long. So there's only room enough for a couple of trees, some old-fashioned lampposts, and a minimal amount of grass, because most of the ground is covered with the engraved bricks that helped raise money for the project.

It was built on the site of an old drugstore that was destroyed by fire. The wall of an adjacent building remained, so it became the west boundary of the park. The bare bricks and mortar are covered by a mural depicting an image of that girl in the flatbed truck, reflected in the window of a hotel. And in the foreground, leaning on his guitar

★ ★

and looking like he wants to be looked at, is a life-size bronze statue of the young man who came to Winslow to stand on a corner.

The citizens of Winslow who first proposed such a park were warned that they'd be the laughingstock of the state if they went ahead with the idea. They went ahead anyway, and now hundreds of tourists get off Interstate 40 to drive here and stand on a corner.

The park is right there at the intersection of Kinsley Avenue and Second Street, on what was once part of the fabled Route 66. Anyone can go there, day or night, and there's no fee for standin'.

Get a New (and Inexpensive) Hairdo
Wupatki National Monument

Many of the tourists who visit Wupatki National Monument are quite likely to roam through the ancient ruins without ever knowing about "the blowhole" because, compared to what else there is to examine and ponder on the grounds, it's minimal to the point of being hardly worth noticing. In fact, it looks more like an unpretentious square sandstone bench than a curiosity.

Located near the ceremonial ball court east of the major sandstone ruins, the blowhole is a crevice in the Earth's crust that creates the impression that it's capable of breathing. It connects to an earth crack, an underground passage formed by earthquake activity in the Kaibab limestone bedrock. The hole reacts to barometric pressure above ground. When the surface air is warm and dry above, the crack blows cold air out with such force that it'll make your hair stand straight up. But when the air gets heavy and moist, it reverses itself and sucks the air downward. And your hair with it. This makes it a place to avoid for those wearing hairpieces and wigs.

Archaeologists have yet to determine what, if any, use the blowhole served for the ancient ones who built the Wupatki complex. Today, the Hopi descendents of the original inhabitants call it "Yaaponsta" (the Wind Spirit). The ruins are about thirty miles northeast of Flagstaff off US Highway 89. For fees and hours, call (928) 679-2365 or check out nps.gov/wupa.

Carrie Nelson gets her hair dried for free at the blowhole in Wupatki National Monument.

Staying Aloft the Hard Way

Yuma

An old airplane dubbed the *City of Yuma* has been painstakingly restored and given a permanent home here. It's an Aeronca Sedan AC15 that once helped the city get through a tough financial crisis by spending more than one thousand consecutive hours airborne.

In 1949, while Yuma was suffering from a postwar economic depression, several local businessmen came up with the idea that an

★ ★

endurance flight would thrust the community into the international spotlight. They got sponsors, volunteers, and donors to provide the plane, the refueling car, and their time. Then they set out to break the existing record.

The plane had to be rigged to handle extra fuel and supplies, and the refueling car, a 1949 Buick convertible, was outfitted with a platform on the back. The volunteers would stand on the platform and pass the necessities to the plane flying a mere three feet overhead while both were roaring down the runway at more than seventy miles per hour.

The first two attempts failed due to trouble with the plane. But the project was finally launched successfully on August 24, 1949. Pilots Woody Jongeward and Bob Woodhouse took four-hour turns at the controls, then slept or made adjustments and repairs on the plane. They had to maneuver the aircraft over the Buick twice a day to make the exchanges. The fuel was handed up to the non-flying pilot in two-and-a-half-gallon cream cans, and the plane-to-car handoffs had to be exact or the vehicles would collide.

There was also the problem of going potty. Prior to the flight, the ground crew furnished a small aluminum pot and some waterproof bags. Woodhouse said that "whenever you got whatever you wanted into that pot, then you'd pull up the bag and twist the little wire around the top, and then we'd fly over California and throw it out 'cause we had heard they needed the water over there."

The pair stayed aloft until October 10. They flew 89,920 miles while establishing a world record of 1,124 hours (more than forty-seven days) before landing in front of twelve-thousand-plus spectators and cheering fans. The stunt was covered by international news media and may have been instrumental in creating an economic upturn that followed. But their endurance record endured for less than ten years. Two Nevada pilots stayed aloft for more than sixty-four days from December 1958 to February 1959.

The airplane was later sold and wound up in Minnesota. In the early 1990s, the Yuma Jaycees spearheaded a project to buy it and return it to the scene of its former glory. After it was restored, the plane was kept at the Yuma Airport until the spring of 2012, when it was moved to its new home in Yuma City Hall. The twelve-hundred-pound aircraft can be seen suspended from the ceiling in the main lobby.

Not a Wham-Bam Incident

The arid desert south of Thatcher in Graham County was the site of the historic Wham Paymaster Robbery, which, despite the name, had nothing to do with "wham," "bam" or any of those other common Batman terms.

It's so named because on May 11, 1889, a gang of robbers ambushed a group of soldiers carrying a US Army payroll to Fort Thomas, and Major Thomas W. Wham was in charge of the unit. After a lengthy gun battle, the outlaws made off with $28,345.10 in gold and silver coins.

Eleven men were arrested in connection with the robbery; only seven stood trial in federal court. But despite overwhelming evidence against them, most of it from testimony delivered by the soldiers, all of the defendants were found not guilty and none of the money was ever recovered.

Major Wham was held accountable for the loss of the payroll until a military tribunal exonerated him. No one else was ever charged.

For details, read the account written by Larry T. Upton, "Robbing the US Army: Facts and Folklore Behind the Wham Paymaster Robbery," at wham.org/UptonRob.htm.

★ ★

An Almost Sure Thing
Yuma

This city is so proud of its sunshine that it has always been willing to bet on it. And with good reason. According to the Guinness World Records, Yuma is the sunniest place on the face of planet Earth, with blue or partially blue skies prevailing an average of 4,055 hours out of a possible 4,456 daytime hours every year. That's 91 percent of the time.

More than a century ago, Yuma hotels backed up the sunshine boasts by offering free board to visitors every day the sun didn't shine. Times have changed, but every now and then, the city comes up with some new sunshine-related freebies. For example, to help celebrate Arizona's centennial, participating restaurants offered complimentary meals for registered guests at participating hotels every time the sun didn't break through. The promotion lasted a year, from August 1, 2011, to July 30, 2012. Full sunshine wasn't required; it counted as a sunny day if the sun came out bright enough for a while so you could see your shadow.

Provisions were in place in case there was a completely non-sun day. That rarity would be declared "Code Gloom" by a committee composed of tourist bureau staffers and local meteorologists, and it would be officially announced when hotels placed a life-sized cutout of Mayor Alan Krieger in their lobbies.

It never happened.

The city went an entire year without giving away a free meal because nobody saw their shadow. And, according to Yuma's media relations specialist Ann Walker, no groundhogs were harmed during the promotion.

An Unclear Verdict

Phoenix

The "Great Soul Trial" of 1967 had nothing to do with tryouts for a gospel singing group. Instead, it was a legal attempt to prove the existence of a human soul. And, not surprisingly, there was a lot of money involved.

The unusual court case had its beginnings in 1949, when a seventy-year-old prospector named James Kidd disappeared in the wilderness of the Superstition Mountains east of Phoenix. He was eventually declared dead, but then, years later, someone discovered that Kidd had left more than two hundred thousand dollars in cash and investments. He had also left a will that declared all his money should go to "a research or some scientific proof of a soul in the human body which leaves at death."

After the will was filed for probate in 1964, the case was heard in Maricopa County Superior Court in Phoenix in 1967. About 140 soul-searchers laid claim to the inheritance, but the money was awarded to Barrow Neurological Institute, a well-known neuro-research lab in Phoenix.

However, others appealed the decision, and in 1973 Kidd's fortune was given to the American Society of Psychical Research in New York, which was founded in 1885 to investigate spiritual phenomena and other things of that nature. The society accepted the money, and then spent it on the study of out-of-body experiences and deathbed revelations. In the end, all the group's findings were inconclusive.

About the only certainties that came out of it all were that the money was gone, and that Kidd never came back to complain about the way it was spent.

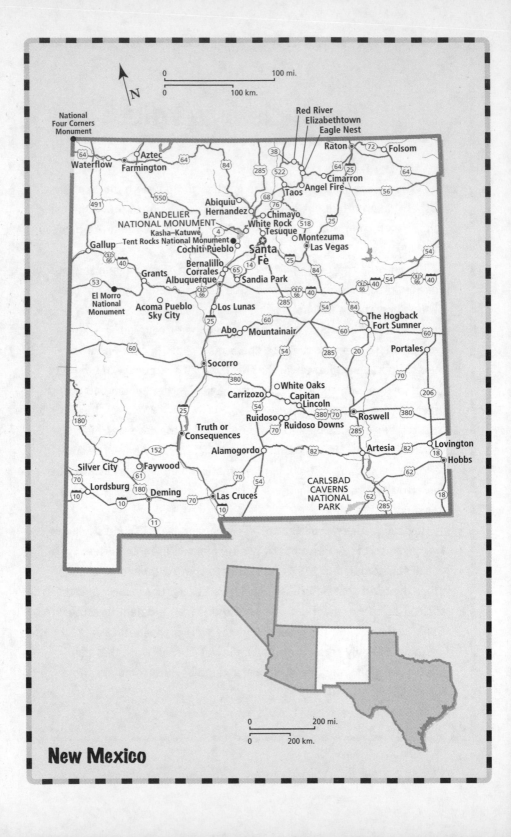

New Mexico

3

New Mexico

While traveling across New Mexico, I've visited places with names like Friendly Village, Hometown USA, Nice 'n' Easy, Handshake Hills, Welcome Vista, and Howdy Pard. These unique monikers divulge that New Mexico is not only the Land of Enchantment, it is also a scenic enrichment with a down-home attitude and a curious collection of curious things.

It's filled with wonderful oddities that give it even more appeal, especially to those who seek out the unusual. From Lordsburg to Clayton, from Jal to Shiprock, from Hobbs to Albuquerque, and Chama to Las Cruces, every inquiry about things of a weird nature is greeted with sincere offers to help.

While Roswell's much-publicized UFO incident may get most of the attention, those who end their search for the odd stuff there will have scraped only the barest surface of the state's weirdness. Those who pursue their quest for the out-of-the-ordinary further will find residents who use emptied beer bottles to build houses, an artist who turned garbage into a giant roadrunner, a man who built a blue elephant to settle an election bet, a place where a single tree constitutes a forest, and grown-ups who enjoy playing in the mud.

The state is home to buildings that resemble a half-inflated hot air balloon and an upside-down chocolate Dixie Cup. Within its borders are giant rocks with tent-like features, murals painted on water tanks, centuries-old graffiti, and a place called Hogback.

★ ★

Billy the Kid's legacy is closely connected to New Mexico, but the state has many lesser-known icons, like William McDonald, whose memorial looks like a giant spider; John Mutz, who built a dragon to watch over his fields; Ansel Adams, whose one-shot photograph became a national treasure; and Bill Dalley, who collects old windmills.

Because of all those elements, coupled with its spectacular scenery and unparalleled friendship, New Mexico is worth a multitude of return visits for anyone seeking the delightful combination of the serene and the curious.

Cast in Stone

Abiquiu

People who search the world for curious rock formations will find an El Dorado here because nature sculpted a variety of masterpieces into boulders, limestone, tuff, and sandstone in this area, then hid them in the surrounding hills. The weirdest is El Pedernal, a huge boulder that balances on a rock spire in such a precarious position that those who find it must wonder how much Super Glue it took to hold it in place. It's about one mile to the north off US Highway 84 as it passes through Abiquiu, but it's somewhat difficult to reach because the road is dirt, unmarked, and not very straight, so it's best to stop and ask for directions.

A few miles to the west, also off US Highway 84, huge chunks of limestone and white sandstone rise dramatically from the surrounding high desert. The place is called Plaza Blanca and the formations resemble Grecian temples. Some of them are more than one hundred feet high, and they're relatively easy to reach by taking the Rio Arriba County Road 155 about six miles northwest off US Highway 84, turning north through a large gate made of telephone poles, and then turning right where the dirt road meets pavement.

The land is privately owned but visitors are welcome as long as they don't climb on the rocks, wander off the designated trails, or take photographs for commercial use.

And then, about sixteen miles west of Plaza Blanca and right on US Highway 84, the Echo Canyon Amphitheater causes a lot of head turning and brake squealing because it looks so inviting. It's also sandstone, but the colors change as they scale up the sides, from red to yellow to white, sort of like somebody plopped a big scoop of spumoni ice cream on the spot and left it there to harden.

It's a large hollow, probably big enough to hold the Mormon Tabernacle Choir, a full orchestra, and a good-size crowd. It's on National Forest Service land so there's an admission fee, but photo buffs can stop, drool, and take pictures from the entry road at no cost.

★ ★

Strange rock formations abound in and around Abiquiu.

Because some of the formations are hard to find, it's best to stop at the Tin Moon Studio and Gallery in Abiquiu and ask for a free map. The studio is on the south side of US Highway 84, right behind the post office. Abiquiu is about twenty-three miles northwest of Espanola on US Highway 84, in the midst of the Santa Fe National Forest. For more information, call (505) 685-4829.

Aren't Those Things Supposed to Be Pink?

Abo

An old elephant stands alongside the road out in the midst of nowhere, mournfully watching the traffic pass by. It's basic blue with touches of yellow, red, and green. This would seem to be a direct violation of the elephant color code because, as all veterinarians, zoologists, and over-imbibers know, elephants normally come only in gray. Or pink.

A couple of other factors also hint that it probably isn't a real elephant. For one thing, it's been standing on that exact spot for more than forty years. For another thing, it's made of cement. And, as a clincher, it's only about four feet tall at the shoulders instead of the

A lonely blue elephant stands guard on the roadside near Abo.

★ ★

usual elephant size, which is generally somewhere between huge and "Holy head cold! Did you see the snout on that thing?!"

The creature appears to be standing guard at a structure that once served as a restaurant. It was allegedly placed there in the 1960s by a former owner of the property as a result of losing an election bet. Details are sketchy, but according to one source, the principals involved were on different sides of the political fence. One was a Democrat; the other a Republican. They agreed that whoever lost the bet had to put a symbol of the other guy's party on his property. When the Republican's candidate won the election, the Democrat had to install the elephant. Had it turned out the other way, there'd be a cement donkey guarding the lonely spot.

Or so the story goes.

Those interested in psychedelic pachyderms can spot this one on the north side of US Highway 60, about seven miles west of Mountainair.

Not Much Work Here for Loggers
Acoma Pueblo

Under normal circumstances, it would take trained foresters using aerial photography and sophisticated computer software, plus a lot of hours, to count all the growth in a forest. But it's easy to enumerate all the trees in the Acoma National Forest:

Just count to "one," and stop.

Obviously, there's a misnomer here. Forests have acre after acre of trees. The Acoma National Forest consists of a single cottonwood, standing forlornly next to a waterhole on top of a mesa. Also obviously, it's not a real forest. It's simply the name the residents of the pueblo jokingly use when they refer to the lonesome tree.

There were three trees when the "forest" was initially planted several years ago, next to a natural basin that collects rainwater. The other two didn't make it, but the survivor has toughed it out in a very unlikely and unnatural habitat. The pueblo sits on top of a

* *

375-foot-tall mesa and the tree is about the only plant life growing there. Even weeds can barely eke out an existence on the platform because it's actually a big piece of sandstone.

Because of its location, Acoma Pueblo is perhaps better known as "Sky City." It was established atop the mesa about two thousand years ago and claims to be the oldest continuously inhabited community in North America, although villages in Florida and Arizona also make the same statement. Besides the "forest," visitors may also inspect adobe houses, plazas, and the San Esteban del Rey Mission,

A lone tree is facetiously known as the Acoma National Forest.

★ ★

completed about 1640. However, all guests must be accompanied by
an Acoma guide, and photographers need a special permit.

In 2007, Acoma Pueblo was designated a National Trust Historic
Site. A year earlier, the pueblo opened the Sky City Cultural Center
and Haak'u Museum, a 3,500-square-foot tourist center that gives visitors some insight into the native culture. To get there, take exit 108
off Interstate 40 and drive south on US Highway 23/Pareje Drive for
about twelve miles. Details are available at acomaskycity.org or call
(800) 747-0181.

Running Amok in the Muck
Albuquerque

Once every year, certain persons here start thinking dirty.

And playing dirty.

They are participants in a rite of structured uncleanliness known as
the Mudd Volleyball Tournament, held annually to raise money for the
Carrie Tingle Hospital Foundation. The concept is simple: Get a lot of
people together in a big mud hole, give them some volleyballs, and
turn 'em loose.

This form of madness has been going on since 1994 and is now
considered an Albuquerque icon. It draws more than five hundred
teams, who play on eighty-six muddy courts dug into a field off
Broadway Southwest near Rio Bravo. Since the mud is almost knee
deep, such regular volleyball tactics as leaping and spiking are replaced
by sloshing, falling, and getting mud up the nose.

The competition is made even tougher because when volleyballs get
covered with slimy goo, they tend to get slippery and unmanageable.
This, combined with the gunk-filled playing field, calls for completely
different game strategies, including the one that incorporates a return
to the good old days when "here's mud in yer eye" was a common
expression.

The event is held in late June and raises more than three hundred
thousand dollars every year. An estimated twelve thousand spectators

gather round to watch the amateur sloshers and mudders play. Teams entered in past competitions bore such appropriate names as Mudd 'n' Roses, Weapons of Mudd Destruction, and Muddy Amigos.

Got filth on your mind? Call the Albuquerque Convention and Visitors Bureau at (800) 284-2282, or contact the hospital foundation at (505) 243-6626 or check out abqmuddvolleyball.org to see if you're dirty enough to qualify.

A Face in a Tree
Albuquerque

There's a very old cottonwood tree rising from the courtyard next to San Felipe de Neri Church. Ordinarily, it wouldn't draw much attention, other than a casual notation that it's quite large, and the fact that it's on the National Register of Historic Places. But those who walk around the tree and look at the side not visible from the street will spot the figure of a woman clad in blue emerging from the trunk.

It's a wooden statue of the Virgin of Guadalupe, and the figure was actually whittled into the tree trunk. It was carved more than fifty years ago by Toby Avila, a parish member. Avila was on active duty during the Korean Conflict and vowed that if he returned home safely, he would create an image of the Blessed Virgin to show his gratitude.

Using only a kitchen knife and a flashlight, Avila chipped away at the tree trunk for a year before the statue was finished. He had to do the carving and painting at night because he also had a full-time day job. And then, two days after completing the task, Avila died. There was still blue paint on his hands as he lay in state in the sanctuary.

The church, erected in 1793 to replace the original mission built in 1709, is at 2005 North Plaza Street in Old Town Albuquerque, which is off San Felipe Northwest. And since the carving was completed more than a half-century ago, the bark of the tree has grown around portions of it. But the major part remains visible.

To see the sculpture, go through the garden area on the north side of the church and out into the adjacent parking lot.

A grateful Korean War veteran carved a statue of
the Blessed Virgin after returning from battle.

How 'bout Them 'Topes?
Albuquerque

This city has had professional baseball off and on since 1880, and the teams have borne such athletic names as the Browns, the Dukes, the Dons, and the Cardinals. So why, with all the sports-sounding names available, did the current team end up being called the Isotopes?

Isotope isn't a baseball name. An isotope is any of two or more species of atoms of a chemical element with the same atomic number and position on the periodic table and nearly identical chemical behavior but with differing atomic masses and different physical properties. What does any of that have to do with throwing strikes, scratching, running the bases, eating hot dogs, hollering at umpires, and enjoying the seventh-inning stretch?

Blame it on Homer Simpson.

He's a leading character in the popular television cartoon series *The Simpsons,* and he's a rabid fan of a fictional baseball team named the Springfield Isotopes. The owners once threatened to move the team to Albuquerque until Homer went on a hunger strike and ultimately prevented the relocation. So when professional baseball returned to Albuquerque in 2003 after a two-year hiatus, the owners held a Name the Team contest, and sixty-eight thousand fans voted for the Isotopes to easily beat out such other suggestions as Atoms, Dukes, Roadrunners, and 66ers. (Actually, Isotopes isn't such a bad name for an Albuquerque team, considering how much nuclear research is conducted in the immediate area.)

And the public likes the unusual name a whole bunch. Fans across the nation have purchased Isotopes merchandise with such fervor that it is one of the top ten bestsellers in minor league baseball.

The team is affiliated with the Los Angeles Dodgers and plays in the Pacific Coast League. The team mascot is named Orbit; he stands six feet five and weighs three hundred pounds. His favorite TV show is (did you really have to ask?) *The Simpsons*.

There's more of this sci-fi/Simpson/baseball scenario at .albuquerque baseball.com.

Odd-Shaped Buildings
Albuquerque

Not only is Albuquerque the largest city in New Mexico, it is also home to some of the oddest-shaped buildings in the state.

For example, the Anderson-Abruzzo International Balloon Museum houses some big balloons and lots of historical data about big balloons. It's named for Albuquerqueans Maxie Anderson and Ben Abruzzo who, along with Larry Newman, completed the first manned balloon crossing of the Atlantic Ocean in 1978.

It's only natural, then, that the building itself would reflect its contents. The museum was designed to look like a partially inflated hot air balloon, with the entryway representing the mouth of the bag. The interior rises to wondrous heights, just like those big fabric bags do when the hot air is forced into them.

The museum is at 9201 Balloon Museum Drive. For more inflated information, log on to balloonmuseum.com or call (505) 768-6020.

Another example is the Unser Racing Museum, founded by and dedicated to the famous Unser family race car drivers. The building was designed to look like the wheel of a race car. It's round and has six room dividers that represent spokes.

Inside, the floor is made of recycled tires, some of the walls and ceilings resemble checkered flags, the soap dispensers in the men's restroom are shaped like miniature gas pumps, and the conference room is named Jerry's Garage, the name of the Unser family's first automobile-related venture. The Johnny Lightning car that once carried an Unser to victory at Indianapolis revolves in the hub of the giant wheel, and the rooms display other racing cars and some family history.

Those who want to get a sense of how it feels to make left turns while driving two hundred miles miles per hour will find the museum at 1776 Montano Road. For more, visit unserracingmuseum.com or call (505) 341-1776.

And finally, there's El Torreón, a large circular structure that marks the entryway of the National Hispanic Cultural Center. It towers over the surrounding landscape, which is fitting because *torreón* is Spanish for "turret." It stands forty-five feet tall and is painted terra-cotta brown, so it resembles a massive chunk of frozen coffee or chocolate ice cream that slipped from a giant container and landed upside down.

But any such frivolous images vanish once inside the building, where the walls, ceilings, and all other available space are covered with New Mexico artist Frederico Vigil's fresco, a masterpiece that covers 4,300 square feet. Completed in 2012, it traces centuries of Hispanic civilization and three hundred years of Albuquerque history. Vigil, who started the project in 2002, used striking, bold colors to create breath-taking images. Near the top, he painted enormous hands that seem to be reaching inside the tower through a skylight. Halfway down the wall, a Madonna in gold-trimmed vestments stands beside a glowing sun while a newborn babe is lifted toward the heavens.

The tower and cultural center are located at 1701 Fourth Street. For more information, try nhccnm.org and click on the Torreón Fresco, or call (505) 246-2261.

An Unsuccessful Protest
Albuquerque

As protests go, the one here in 1984 was a sort of successful failure. It centered on Debbie Ball, also known as the Candy Lady, and the X-rated confections that saved her business.

Back in the early 1980s, Ball and her mother, Diane Garcia Davis, opened a small candy store and were having a tough time making it. Sales of their eight different kinds of candy weren't what they expected, maintenance was high and, at one point, they considered quitting. Then one day a customer told them about a store in New York that baked and sold naughty sweets, and Ball decided to try that approach. Her mother immediately and strenuously objected, but they reached a compromise—they'd make the X-rated delicacies but keep them in a refrigerator, away from the regular display cases. It was, Ball says now, a big mistake because the new line became such a hit that they almost wore the hinges off the refrigerator door by opening and closing it so often.

Word of the naughty niceties not only spread among her customers, but also reached a church group, who organized a picket line outside her store. Only a couple of picketers appeared on the first day, but as many as 150 showed up the next day. They also asked the city to shut the business down.

But the protest backfired. The *Albuquerque Tribune* ran a front-page story about the incident, and that prompted national media coverage and an offer from the American Civil Liberties Union to defend the store owners. Deluged with so much adverse publicity about their cause, the picketers never came back.

The end result was that Ball and her mom had to work overtime to fill all the requests that came immediately afterward, and the business was saved because of what she said was "three million dollars' worth of free advertising."

Her Candy Lady shop is located at 524 Romero Northwest on the corner of Mountain Road and Rio Grande Boulevard in Old Town (take exit 194 off Interstate 40 and go south). Now she uses more than five thousand different molds to make more than five hundred different types of candy from thousands of recipes. And yes, among them are the ingredients for . . . well . . . you know . . . those items in that special room with the big red X on the door.

Due to a more relaxed attitude toward things of a sexy nature, you don't have to wear a trench coat and fake eyeglasses attached to a big rubber nose when you go into that section of the store. But if you're still uncomfortable, call (505) 243-6239 to place an order and have a liberated friend pick it up. For more information or to order online, visit thecandylady.com.

Here Snowee, Snowee, Snowee
Angel Fire

When November rolls around and the sun's route wanders farther to the south, it is time for the Calling of the Snow, an unofficial function that marks the beginning of the ski season in the southern Rockies of northern New Mexico. The event is held in the parking lot of the Angel Fire Resort and is, according to the people who staff the Tourist Information Center, designed to "invoke the snow gods to give us enough snow for a good ski season."

Participants compete in such categories as loudest call and most unusual call. In the past, they have used old brass horns and kazoos to help their appeals reach the gods of the white stuff. One contestant showed up with a huge alpenhorn; others have used compressed air horns. And yes, some of them actually do holler, "Snowee! Here Snowee!" when it comes to their turn.

The callers and hollerers get backup support from the resort's snow chanters, the beat of their snow drums, and the rhythm of their snow dances. Winners are awarded nominal prizes but the big reward comes with the knowledge that their pleas for white powder are usually answered. Snow has fallen every year since the event began. Of course, it also fell every year *before* the event began.

While all is going on, resort workers ignite a big bonfire and burn an eight-foot effigy of a golfer because the golfing season is over and now it's time for skiing, snowboarding, quaffing rum nog, and other winter sports. And then everybody gathers round the fire to make s'mores.

Angel Fire is about twenty-eight miles east of Taos on US Highway 64, then two miles south on Highway 434. Snow callers and others who wish to cleanse their lungs by bellowing into the clean, crisp mountain air can get more information by calling (800) 633-7463 or checking out angelfireresort.com.

★ ★

Ruminating with a Ruminant

Artesia

Among the items on display at the Artesia Visitors Center and
Chamber of Commerce, located in the magnificently restored Santa
Fe Railroad depot at 107 North First Street (also US Highway 285), is
a cow with a television set in her belly. Her name is Bessie. She's not
a real cow. Real cows actually do put lots of things in their stomachs
because they are ruminants so they can chew their cuds as part of the
digestive process. But even with that advantage, TV sets are not in
their normal diets.

Also, it's a one-channel TV set so those who go there and press
the right button shouldn't expect to see such regular television fare

**A cow with a television set in her tummy
tells a story in Artesia.**

as *Cow I Met Your Mother*, *Cownanza*, or *Holsteinfeld*. Instead, they get to watch a video that relates the history of the dairy industry in the region. It's all part of the Pecos Valley Dairy Museum, also housed in the center. Inside the museum, a digital clock keeps track of how many gallons of milk have been produced in the area since the first of each year.

Those who watch Bessie's tummy and take in the museum often refer to it as an "udderly mooving" experience.

Home of the Nice Soreheads

Aztec

The signs leading into town say WELCOME TO AZTEC. HOME OF 6,378 FRIENDLY PEOPLE AND 6 OLD SOREHEADS. The signs were erected several years ago. Between then and now, the number of friendly people has grown to slightly more than seven thousand, but there are still only six old soreheads.

But being a sorehead in this town is actually an honor, not a denigration. Only residents who have a strong interest in community affairs (and a good sense of humor) can be selected for the dubious distinction. A slate of potential soreheads is announced about midway through the year and the winners are elected by voters who toss coins into their favorite candidate's collection can. Then the six winners get to wear paper sacks over their heads until they are "unveiled" as the new Old Soreheads during an Oktoberfest parade.

To make sure they know how to conduct themselves during their time in office, each sorehead gets a copy of an instruction manual entitled *How to be an Old Sorehead*. It doesn't say anything about grumpiness, grousing around, causing stomach upset, snarling at little children, tipping less than 2 percent, or frowning. Instead, it lists nice things like getting involved in the community and how to help people less fortunate.

The tradition started in 1969 and all the money contributed in the form of votes goes to community projects. But it hasn't always received

★ ★

full support from all the townspeople. Since 1970, city officials (also referred to as "those wet blankets") have made two stabs at getting rid of the tradition and the signs, but have been voted down both times.

The Original High-Rise District
Bandelier National Monument

So you think living in a high-rise apartment makes you a trendsetter? Well, it's actually nothing new and it's not that big a deal. The folks who once resided here were doing it more than seven hundred years ago.

Tourists can scramble around in ancient second-story housing units in Bandelier National Monument.

The ancient Puebloans who settled in the area not only built stone houses and kivas, but also dug caves into the tuff stone that had been deposited by volcanic eruptions more than a million years ago. The caves served as ideal residences and storehouses because they stayed cool in the summer and warm in the winter. Even though the tuff is relatively soft, carving into it was difficult because the carvers had only stone tools.

The lower walls were usually plastered with mud and then painted using native plants as dye. The ceilings, however, were soon blackened by smoke from the cooking and heating fires inside the caves. The smoke hardened the ceilings and made them less crumbly.

Now visitors to the monument can scramble around in the caves, once they pay the entry fee and take a short hike. The first complex was dug into a huge chunk of tuff, and some of the makeshift homes were as much as thirty feet above ground. Access was (and still is) by wooden ladders propped against the openings, but amateur spelunkers should be forewarned of this problem: The ladders are crude, not at all like those on sale at your friendly neighborhood hardware store. The rungs are much farther apart so it takes a series of large steps to reach the top. And then comes the hard part: getting back down. The Old Ones who built the ladders might have been able to scoot up and down without fear, but today's climbers have to make their retreats the same way babies crawl down stairs: backward and very slowly.

The monument is southeast of White Rock on Highway 4. For more information, call (505) 672-3861 or visit nps.gov/band.

A Bar for All Mankind
Bernalillo

The Silva Saloon is one of those places you hear stories about, but you always wonder if they really exist or are merely the illusions visualized by beer-soaked brain cells. This is because bars like this are so one-of-a-kind that when others try to emulate them, they rarely succeed because they have neither the right amount of showmanship, nor the proper number of kitschy—but priceless—artifacts.

It is not so much the bar itself; it's the decor. The bar is a common octagon shape, made of teakwood and aged by decades-old applications of spilled suds, weary elbows, and tales of misunderstanding spouses. A couple of strategically placed peanut dispensers offers sustenance and a friendly barkeep maintains a steady flow of assorted brews and distilled liquids, just like the thousands of other saloons that serve as gathering places for the thirsty, the tired, and the misunderstood.

But the walls, the ceilings, and every other available space are what make the Silva Saloon a curiosity because they are covered with things. Funky stuff, things nobody really needs but would really like to have. Like old license plates and aged lanterns, cowboy boots and baseball caps. Paintings of nude women, old photos, dollar bills, saddles, antique toy cars, a device for administering beer intraveneously, neon signs that still work, life-size pin-ups, jewelry, skulls, canes, bells, old whiskey bottles, pins, and jukeboxes, to name but a few.

The saloon was opened in 1931 by Felix Silva Sr., and is the oldest family-owned bar in New Mexico. It was elevated to a place of high distinction in 2007 when it was named to *Esquire* magazine's list of "Best Bars in America," the only establishment of its kind in the state to be so honored.

Anyone with a hankerin' to take a trip down Memory Lane, put a nickel into a nickelodeon, gaze at an Elvis decanter, or just have a cold beer will find the saloon at 955 Camino del Pueblo in downtown Bernalillo. The phone number is (505) 867-9976.

A Long Way Up—and Down
Carlsbad Caverns

Since Albuquerque is the largest city in New Mexico with more than eight hundred thousand residents, it's logical to assume that Albuquerque would also have the tallest building in the state. And it does. The twenty-two-story Albuquerque Plaza rises 351 feet, earning the tallest designation by a wide margin.

★ ★

And since that's the tallest building in the state, it's thereby logical to assume that it also has the longest elevator shaft in the state. But it doesn't. The elevator that carries tourists from ground level to the primary viewing areas deep inside the Carlsbad Caverns National Park is more than twice as long as any other in all of New Mexico.

It's 750 feet one way, about the same height as a seventy-five-story building. Construction crews worked nearly eight months and used twelve tons of dynamite to blast the shaft in 1931. And the elevator they installed back then is still in use today. It travels at the rate of nine miles per hour, so it takes a minute to go from top to bottom or vice versa.

However, those with claustrophobia may use the Natural Entrance Route, which is longer in both time required and distance traveled. It's a self-guided tour for visitors with plenty of time and it's not recommended for the pot-of-bellied or the weak-of-kneed because it's all downhill one way and all uphill the other way. The one-mile hike traces the traditional explorers' route, and follows steep and narrow trails through a tall trunk passage known as the Main Corridor. Fortunately, it's well worth the extra effort.

Either way, when guests reach the bottom, they'll find what are probably the nation's most subterranean snack bar and gift shop dispensing munchies and souvenirs more than one-sixth of a mile below the surface of the earth.

The park is about twenty-five miles southwest of Carlsbad along US Highway 62/180. For hours and information, call (877) 444-6777 or log on to nps.gov/cave.

A Very Large Four-Legged Non-Spider
Carrizozo

Ask anyone in town where the McDonald Park is located and many of them won't know. But ask them where the Spider Park is, and nearly everyone has the correct answer.

It's a small patch of ground on the east side of the town's main drag as it saunters through the heart of the community. And right in the middle of the park sits the spider. Actually, it's not a real spider, and it was never intended even to be mistaken for a creepy crawly critter. It's a concrete and lava rock sculpture that may have originally been designed as a fountain. Now they call it a monument. It has four arches that connect a large rock cupola in the center. That, coupled with the dark brown coloration of lava rock, gives it a tarantula-like appearance because the arches look like legs and the cupola looks like a spider body. A very big spider body.

In reality, the park was named for William C. McDonald, New Mexico's first governor after statehood. He served from 1912 to 1917. Although very few can recall what made McDonald famous, his park must be held in some degree of reverence because there's a sign warning that would-be spider riders can be fined as much as one hundred dollars for climbing on the stone creature.

Big-time arachnid hunters will find this giant on US Highway 54 as it goes through Carrizozo, about fifty-two miles north of Alamogordo. Those truly interested in the park's actual namesake will find his gravesite in White Oaks, a near-ghost town twelve miles northeast of Carrizozo on Highway 349.

The Holiness of Dirt
Chimayo

Most of the wall space in the sacristy of El Santuario del Chimayo is covered with icons, pictures, and other religious symbols. But one section appears to have nothing to do with religion. It's a row of crutches and braces hanging from racks attached to the wall. The reason for this curiosity becomes perfectly clear upon learning about the history and legend of the little church.

The small adobe structure is frequently referred to as "the Lourdes of the Southwest" because, like the shrine in France where the faithful believe the Blessed Virgin Mary visited St. Bernadette, it is said to be

Legend says the dirt from the floor of Santuario del Chimayo has wrought miracles.

responsible for miraculous cures. And the crutches and other medical devices here, like those at Lourdes, were placed by the people who left their afflictions behind.

The stories of the miracles center around a small hole in the ground in a room off to the side of the altar. Many believe that the dirt from the floor of the sanctuary (called *tierra bendita* or "sacred earth") has curative powers, so pilgrims remove small portions from the hole, aided by a couple of little tin shovels left there for such a purpose.

The origins of the legend go back to the Tewa Indians, some of the first inhabitants of the area. Later, Spanish settlers propagated the belief that the ground was sacred by recalling miracles, and a shrine was erected on the spot in 1758 when an archbishop claimed he had been cured of a contagious disease after a visit.

Around 1810, according to another part of the legend, a friar saw a light beaming from a hillside, so he dug into the spot and recovered a crucifix. The icon was taken to a nearby town but it disappeared. The friar found it and returned it to the village. It disappeared again. The holy man recovered it, returned it to the village, and it vanished again. Eventually, the crucifix was found back in its original site. Believing this to be a sign from above, the people built a small chapel there. Miraculous healing began shortly thereafter at that spot and became so numerous that the chapel had to be replaced by the larger, current Chimayo Shrine. It was built in 1816 and is still very much in its original condition.

Chimayo is located about forty miles northeast of Santa Fe. Take US Highway 285 north out of Santa Fe to Highway 76, and then drive about four miles east. The little church is in the heart of the community, sitting in a verdant area so beautiful that even skeptics should find a degree of peace and contentment there.

For more information, visit holychimayo.us.

Wild and Woolly

Cimarron

Cimarron means "wild" or "unruly" in Spanish, and twenty-one bullet holes in the hammered tin ceiling of the St. James Hotel support the idea that it was a suitable name for the town back in the 1880s. Because it was a vital outpost on the old Santa Fe Trail, the St. James was a gathering place for several of history's more unsavory characters, including Jesse James and Bob Ford, the guy who shot Jesse in the back.

Twenty-six men were killed in or in front of the St. James. One of them was Davy Crockett II, nephew of the more famous Davy

Crockett. He was mortally wounded in a gunfight on the street that runs past the hotel. Clay Allison also hung out there. A plaque on one wall claims he killed nineteen men and lists them by name, and it's said he also danced naked on the bar and was responsible for several of the overhead bullet holes. Ironically, although he was a feared gunman, Allison met his demise when he fell off a farm wagon in Texas.

Other famous, or infamous, hotel guests included Buffalo Bill Cody and Annie Oakley, who met in the bar, Bat Masterson, Lucien Maxwell, Kit Carson, Billy (the Kid) Bonney, and Henri Lambert, personal chef to President Abraham Lincoln and, in 1872, founder of the saloon that evolved into the St. James Hotel.

Today's guests are of a more gentle demeanor. They eat in the Carson-Maxwell Dining Room, take liquid refreshment in the Lambert Saloon, and spend the nights in one of the fourteen rooms still in use. But, as sort of a tribute to those wilder times on the frontier, there are no television sets or telephones in the rooms. However, the punctured tin ceilings have never been repaired so the bullet holes are still there as permanent reminders of a notorious past.

The hotel is located on Highway 21 about a half-mile south of US Highway 64, which serves as the town's main drag. For details, call (888) 376-2664 or go to exstjames.com.

The Fine Art of Mudding
Corrales

New Mexico is one of the select places on the planet where mudding is a team sport. It's because there are so many adobe buildings across the state and frequently (in general, once a year) they have to be remudded.

Mudding is an art that has been practiced ever since humans learned how to make structures with adobe bricks. Because the bricks are essentially mud, they have to be remudded so they don't wash away when it rains. But because average annual rainfall in most of New Mexico is rather limited, the buildings hold up well, provided they get regular muddings.

✦ ✦

Casa San Ysidro in Corrales is one such target of mudding crews. The old house, now a part of the Albuquerque Museum, hosts *Dia de Enjarrar* (Mudding Day) once a year. More than thirty volunteers show up for the event, during which they learn how to mix and apply the goopy stuff. For the most part, it's done the same way people have been doing it for centuries. They do, however, make one concession to mechanization by using a heavy-duty electric mixer to make the mud. The recipe is quite simple:

25 shovels full of dirt
15 shovels full of sand
2 handfuls of hay, crumbled to an inch or two in length
About 5 ounces of bonding adhesive, if necessary
Enough water to make it smooth and thick

Once mixed, scoop the mud into buckets and use a special trowel when applying it to the existing surface that has been sprayed with water so it bonds with the new mud. If the mix is good, the mud adheres perfectly. A bad batch, however, won't be compatible and big chunks will fall off. Let dry. Repeat next year.

Casa San Ysidro is located at 973 Old Church Road in Corrales. Volunteers interested in mud-application duty with a serious overtone can get information by calling (505) 898-3915.

Running Ducks, Flying Tortillas, and Speedy Outhouses
Deming

So what's a city to do when it's suddenly faced with economic disaster?

Turn the situation over to the ducks, of course.

Deming did, and it worked wonders.

In the late 1970s, a shirt factory that had been a major employer in Deming shut down, putting the city in a bit of a crisis mode. A group of businessmen held discussions on how to counteract the factory's demise and came up with (and this is for real, folks) duck races.

Athletic ducks take center stage once every year in Deming.

Get some ducks, build some racing pens, and turn 'em loose.
Ducky.
Just plain ducky.
The first one was held in 1980 and it was a triumph beyond anyone's expectations, attracting not only duck-racing fans but also
national and international media attention. And in sort of a storybook
ending, the second-place finisher in the first Great American Duck
Race was Robert Duck, a duck racer from Bosque Farms. Duck's ducks
went on to win the event for several years after that before he ducked
out of the competition.

★ ★

The first races were for running ducks only, but now there's also a race for swimming ducks that paddle in water-filled lanes just like the Olympians do, except the ducks don't wear Speedos.

In addition, the annual festivities now include the Great American Tortilla Toss and the Great American Outhouse Race in which three-person teams careen through the streets in vehicles designed to look like what used to be blushingly referred to as "the little house out behind the big house."

Of course, there's also a Tournament of Ducks Parade and a Great American Duck Royalty Pageant in which contestants in various age groups waddle around the stage dressed like ducks under the supervision of (get this) the Quackmaster.

For more, log on to demingduckrace.com or call (888) 345-1125. Just don't make any wisequacks.

Spray-Paintless Graffiti
El Morro National Monument

Those who assume that graffiti followed the invention of felt-tip markers and aerosol paint cans will be in for a bit of a surprise if they visit the El Morro National Monument, where the names scrawled on the walls are hundreds of years old. And not only that, the works of those taggers are protected by the federal government, primarily because of their age.

Although the rock formation now known as *El Morro* (the headland) was created way back in antiquity, the first recorded mention of the site occurred in 1583 when some Spanish soldiers stopped for water and noted the site in their journals. For the next three hundred years, hundreds of Spaniards passed the spot and many of them carved their names into the soft sandstone and limestone. Next came American soldiers, settlers, emigrants, freighters, and explorers, and many of them also left their marks.

The oldest, and most famous, example of this form of penmanship was hammered into the rock in 1605 by the first governor of the

Centuries-old etchings mark some of the rocks
at El Morro National Monument.

territory. He wrote (or chiseled): "Passed by here the Governor Don
Juan do Onate from the discovery of the Sea of the South on the 16th
of April, 1605." That was fifteen years before the pilgrims landed at
Plymouth Rock.

The brochures handed out at the monument's visitor center give
this explanation for why people perform such defacing acts: "Perhaps
it was the notion of immortality—an inspiration for creative endeavors
since the dawn of the human race—that compelled people to write

their own lives into rock. Compared to our life spans, El Morro is timeless."

Anyone interested in seeing how graffiti artists "decorated" before spray paint was invented can reach El Morro by driving south and west for about forty miles on Highway 53 out of Grants (off Interstate 40, take exit 81 or 81A.) For details, log onto nps.gov/elmo or call (505) 783-4226.

Keeping the Prairie Safe
Elizabethtown

There's not much town left here. But E-Town, as the locals call it, was at one time a booming community created by miners who dug riches from the ground, spent the riches in local saloons and brothels, and then left once the good times ended.

A steel dragon keeps a watchful eye out for knights in shining armor near Elizabethtown.

* *

Or, more romantically, maybe the people left because of the dragon.

Well, probably not. The people were gone long before the dragon showed up.

He's impressive, though, looking fierce while sitting out there in the middle of a pasture. But he's just your typical dragon: green head, red eyes, red nose, big jaws, mean expression. Only his head and tail are visible; the rest of his body is hiding underground, apparently waiting to digest the remains of the unwary passerby who gets too close.

But he's not an actual threat because he's composed of steel culverts, not fire and brimstone, the usual dragon components. John Mutz, a member of a prominent ranching family in the Moreno Valley, built him in the 1980s as a parade float for a Fourth of July celebration in Red River. Once the festivities were over, Mutz took the dragon back to his ranch and buried its midsection, thereby converting the beast into a culvert.

Knights in shining armor looking for a challenge can spot the creature on the west side of Highway 38 about six miles north of Eagle Nest. There are no signs marking the dragon's lair so it takes keen eyes to spot it. Those who do can pull off the road onto an approach and walk about twenty feet to a gate in the fence that surrounds the field guarded by the fake fire-snorter. But the land is posted so go no farther. Unless, of course, you have no fear of either dragons or irate ranchers who might discourage trespassers with buckshot.

Look! Up in the Sky! It's a Trucksicle!
Farmington

The landscape along the main highway east of Farmington is relatively flat, an element that makes the truck-on-a-stick stand out. Or stick out.

It's a 1928 Model A Ford pickup truck perched atop a fifty-foot steel tower in front of Moberg Welding, Inc. John Moberg, the owner, hoisted it up there in 2001 to attract attention. It works. It's visible for several miles in all directions, making it hard to miss even if you're not watching the skies for UFOs.

A high-rise pickup truck gets plenty of
attention near Farmington.

★ ★

The old truck had been sitting around the shop yard for years before Moberg welded it to the steel pipe and hired a crane operator to raise it skyward. He said it's under the FAA height limit, so he didn't have to install a strobe light to warn low-flying aircraft that there's a Model A in their flight path.

But some words of caution for those who drive by: Look out while you're looking up. There may be someone coming from the opposite direction who has also taken eyes off the road to gawk at the trucksicle.

The welding shop is east of town at 5837 US Highway 64 on the south side of the road, about a half-mile beyond the intersection of US Highway 64 and Crouch Mesa Road/Highway 350.

A Mighty Flush
Faywood

There are times when something off in the distance looks so real that it's almost like seeing a mirage. This happens northwest of Deming, when the City of Rocks State Park pops into view and takes on the appearance of a major city rising up in the middle of nowhere.

But the things that look like skyscrapers are actually rocks. Big rocks. Very big rocks. From a couple of miles away, however, they resemble a cityscape, especially to those cartoon fans who once watched Fred Flintstone and Barney Rubble cavort around Bedrock City.

Technically, the rocks are volcanic deposits—basalt, andresite, and rhyolite—that were spewed up from inner earth more than thirty million years ago. When the lava hardened, erosion sculpted the forms that appear today.

Some look like mushrooms, others like embracing couples and human faces. But the main attraction sits right next to the park entrance. Viewed from any angle, it appears to be a giant toilet.

★ ★

The place to go is this toilet-shaped rock in City of Rocks State Park.

To get to the park, take US Highway 180 north out of Deming
for 23 miles, turn east on Highway 61 and drive about three miles
to the site. For more information, visit emnrd.state.nm.us/SPD/cityof
rocksstatepark.html or call (505) 536-2800.

Dollars in the Antlers
Folsom

There's a small fortune hanging on the walls of the saloon at the
Folsom Village Inn. The treasure contains thousands of pieces, and
almost every piece is a one-dollar bill. They're everywhere—stapled

to the walls, pinned to the ceiling, the walls, and the bar itself, and impaled on the antlers of a stuffed deer head that stares down on the saloon patrons.

This all started almost thirty years ago, when Mercedes and Richard Phillips opened the combination bar, restaurant, and lodging establishment. Mrs. Phillips pinned the first dollar the couple made to the wall, and patrons thought it was such a novel idea that they started doing likewise.

Some of the bills are autographed and some are foreign. And some big spenders have left their marks in the form of larger bills. But before you get ready to go rid the place of its riches, consider this: After a few years of serving as decor, the bills begin to deteriorate. "They just fall apart," said Tanya Garcia, a granddaughter of the founders and current owner of the place. She attributes it to cigarette smoke and kitchen residue. "We let them hang there until they rot away," she added. "We don't count them anymore, but at one time there were about thirty-five hundred of them."

That's thirty-five hundred bucks. Or, in more recognizable terms, that's about fourteen hundred beers.

Got an extra dollar that's just itching to be hung someplace where everybody will see it and comment that they've never heard of you? The Folsom Village Inn is waiting on Highway 325. Investors and others can get more information by calling (575) 278-2478. And while you're waiting to make sure the thumbtack or piece of used bubble gum is holding your contribution firmly in place, you can order a Folsom burger, one of the house specialties.

You Want Fries with That Three-Foot Bullet?

Fort Sumner

The Red Bandana Cafe has a novel way of attracting customer attention—perceived overkill.

The eatery has a big six-shooter stationed near its front door. It's huge. It's even bigger than that. It's enormous. The thing is about ten

★ ★

A huge six-shooter invites diners into a restaurant in Fort Sumner.

feet long and stands about five feet tall, and the ammunition cylinder looks as if it could hold a half-dozen three-foot cartridges.

But even though the legend of Billy the Kid is still told and retold over and over in the area, it's not a real gun. It's a barbecue grill. It hasn't been used to turn steers into dinner for several years, however, and now it just sits there, threatening to blast a three-foot hole into anyone who doesn't stop for lunch or dinner.

The cafe is on the south side of US Highway 60 at 1535 East Sumner Avenue, the town's main street. For more information on the possibility of getting blasted, call (575) 355-9464.

★ ★

Four-State Contortions
Four Corners National Monument

Some tourists say they go to the Four Corners National Monument because it's the only place in the United States where four states meet. But many of those who make that claim aren't being completely honest. The real reason they make the trip is to have their picture taken while standing in four states at the same time. And because of that, it's also a paradise for photographers who like to take pictures of people contorting themselves into weird shapes while smiling at the camera and saying "cheese."

The four states meet at the intersection of a large X traced into a concrete slab. Through some strategic—but not necessarily graceful—placement of feet and hands, visitors can stand in New Mexico, Arizona, Colorado, and Utah at the same time. (Those who manage to perform the maneuver will notice that weather conditions and scenery are pretty much the same in all four.)

Several methods are used to achieve the four-states-at-one-time positioning. The most common is the four-state squat, placing a foot in two quadrants, then a hand in the other two. More adventuresome state counters will also employ the quad-state plop, a technique in which they simply flop down over the X and wave their arms and legs like a kid making a snow angel. Others go through gyrations that vaguely resemble dancing at a singles club, or somebody doing a bad impersonation of a four-legged tarantula.

The monument is located on US Highway 160 in the far northwestern corner of New Mexico.

And the far northeastern corner of Arizona.

And the far southeastern corner of Utah.

And the far southwestern corner of Colorado.

There's an entry fee, but it's well worth it for those who like to watch people pretzelize themselves. For more information, log on to mesaverde.com/fcmonument.htm.

★ ★

Something Really Big
Gallup

Millions of passersby have taken quick glances at the *Paso por Aqui* sculpture as they motor through Gallup in either direction on Interstate 40, but most will only wonder what it is because they don't take the time to stop and inquire.

For them: Here are some answers.

The name means "pass through here," and it's a tribute to the many groups of people who played roles in the city's history: Native Americans, miners, railroad crews, ranchers, settlers, and all the others.

Pasa por Aqui rises above Gallup
and acts like a landmark.

Although it looks like a thirty-foot circle from the freeway, it's actually a loop because the ends never meet to form a complete circle. One end emerges from the base to represent those who first came here, and the other end is a replica of a single railroad track.

Toward the end of the twentieth century, artists Charles Mallery and Robert Hymer were hired by the Cultural Corridors Public Art on Scenic Highways Commission to create the big arch. Or loop. Or circle. Regardless of what it is, the sculpture is on Maloney Avenue between Pueblo and Grandview.

A Second That Lasts Forever
Hernandez

It was toward dusk on October 31, 1941, and photographer Ansel Adams was driving along US Highway 84 when he spotted what he considered an ideal photo op: darkening skies, a full moon, white crosses in a cemetery, a little white church, and clouds. Adams screeched his car to a stop, hauled his camera to a nearby hilltop, and began yelling at his assistants to bring more of his equipment. They couldn't find his exposure meter, which was invaluable because his large camera didn't have one built in, but he figured out the moon's luminescence and quickly took the shot.

One click of the camera.

One single photo.

He wanted to take another but the available light moved faster than he did, and the moment was gone. However, the one image he did capture has taken on a life of its own. It eventually became entitled *Moonrise, Hernandez, New Mexico, 1941*.

Adams said later that it was "certainly my most popular image" because it "combined serendipity and immediate technical recall." Later, he added that "serendipity is just another word for lucky." He made several prints from the single negative and sold them for as little as fifty dollars.

But that was only the beginning.

Today, the photo is a classic. It has appeared on more than two million posters, and prints made from the original negative sell for as much as $70,000. In 1981, one went for $71,500. In 2006, an original sold for a whopping $606,600 at a Sotheby's auction in New York.

The San Jose Catholic Church that appears in the photo is still there, but a newer, larger church has been erected nearby. They're both just off US Highway 84 between mileposts 194 and 195. Hernandez is located where Highways 84 and 74 intersect, about five miles north of Española.

It's a Coca-Cola Thing
Hobbs

Those who enter Casey's, a restaurant owned and operated by Paula Manis, might find it hard to believe that she doesn't drink any more Coca-Cola than the average person because she is a Coke collector of the highest order.

Casey's is a veritable museum that houses the Coca-Cola memorabilia Mrs. Manis has been amassing since 1986. And it's more than Coke bottles. She has every Coca-Cola village ever produced, along with all the people. She has the Coke ads that appeared in *National Geographic* from the 1930s through the 1970s. She has Super Bowl Coke bottles, March Madness Coke bottles, and more than two hundred Coke puzzles.

The windows of her restaurant feature the Coca-Cola polar bears and Coca-Cola Christmas tableaus. She has Coke dispensing machines, including one that was left to her in the will of a woman who wanted to give it to Mrs. Manis instead of to her own children. She doesn't keep a precise count of her artifacts but estimates there are more than five thousand Coke-related items in the four rooms of her eatery, plus another seven boxes of stuff she can't put on display because there's no more space. Among the stuff in the boxes are Coke playing cards, marbles, cigarette lighters, ashtrays, paper dolls, and bottles bearing the logos of professional athletic teams. "People just keep bringing Coke stuff in," Mrs. Manis said. "And we take anything."

"Anything" includes Coke place mats, Coke napkins, and Coke writing instruments.

Caffeine lovers and others can find Casey's at 209 West Broadway or get more information online at eatcaseys.com. And anyone who has an old Coca-Cola washing machine or Coke log cabin they want to donate can call (575) 393-0308. Just try not to burp into the phone.

So . . . Are the Hogback Suburbs Called Piggybacks?

Hogback

Even if you examine a map of New Mexico under a microscope, you won't find a town named Hogback because it's more of a formation than a town. Besides that, there's not much there. Just a trading post, a convenience store, a laundry, and a church. It's hard to miss Hogback, however, due to the looming presence that gives the place its name.

It's a tremendously large hunk of sandstone rising mightily out of the ground, part of a geological formation that runs from Canada to Mexico. Pieces of the formation pop up in New Mexico, Colorado, and Montana, but most of it lies beneath the Earth's surface, sort of like that monster that supposedly swims around in Loch Ness. It has been called a "hogback" since the late 1800s, when the first Anglo settlers arrived and decided it needed to be called something, just on general principles. Then those who came later decided it was an appropriate designation so they named everything else Hogback: the Hogback Trading Post, Hogback Grocery Store, Hogback Laundry, and Hogback Church of Christ.

The place with the romantic name is on US Highway 64, just a couple of miles west of Waterflow. And for those who insist on being technical, Hogback is actually part of Waterflow.

It's worth a stop because of the trading post that has been sitting

**A huge chunk of stone rising from the
ground gives Hogback its name.**

on the same spot for more than 125 years. Founded by Joseph
Wheeler in 1871, it has the distinction of being the oldest trading post
in the nation still operated by the founder's family. Over the years, it
has also served as a bank, mercantile store, and livestock brokerage
institution. Current owner Tom Wheeler maintains a plentiful collection
of traditional and modern Navajo rugs, paintings, silver jewelry, and
alabaster art in a hogan-shaped building that contains ten thousand
square feet of display area.

The address is 3221 Highway 64 and you can usually talk with a
member of the family by calling (505) 598-5154.

A Stone Encampment
Kasha-Katuwe Tent Rocks National Monument

It is not uncommon for first-time visitors to look at the rock formations here and make witty observations like, "That must have been some pow wow!" Or, "Did rock people live in those rock tents?"

They are uneducated, tongue-in-cheek observations, but somewhat understandable. The rocks that give the place its Anglo name are shaped like giant tepees that were pitched and then left out in the sun too long so they turned gray and got rock hard. None of this has anything to do with reality, of course.

Strange rock formations look like they were abandoned by stone campers.

The cone-shaped hoodoos are the products of volcanic eruptions that occurred more than six million years ago and left pumice, ash, and tuff deposits more than one thousand feet thick. Over the millennia, the erosion process has erased much of the original deposit, leaving only the tents. None of them is hollow, however, which rules out the possibility that this was once the site of an enormous encampment of prehistoric tent dwellers.

Some of the formations are topped by boulder caps that temporarily protect them from further erosion. Others have lost their lids and are now being eaten away by the elements, although not fast enough so anybody's going to notice.

The name *Kasha-Katuwe* (white cliffs) comes from the traditional Keresan language of the Cochiti Pueblo that surrounds the monument, located on the Pajarito Plateau. It's considered a remarkable outdoor research laboratory where sites reflecting human occupation spanning four thousand years have been uncovered. During the fourteenth and fifteenth centuries, several large pueblos were established here and the descendants of the builders still inhabit the surrounding area.

Campers who want to experience rock-hard accommodations can reach the monument by taking Highway 22 off Interstate 25 at exit 259 and then following the road to the Cochiti Pueblo, where a right turn leads to the entrance.

Some Very Large Beep-Beepers
Las Cruces (and Alamogordo)

Since the roadrunner is New Mexico's official state bird, it seems only natural that New Mexico should be the home to a couple of the world's largest roadrunners. And so it is.

The biggest one measures about fifteen feet tall and thirty feet long, and it peers down on Las Cruces from atop a mesa at a rest stop on the south side of Interstate 10 on the western edge of the city. What makes it more of an oddity is that it's also a recycling project. In other words, it's made of garbage.

The world's largest roadrunner near Las Cruces
was rescued from a landfill.

Students in a high school welding class created
this huge roadrunner.

The framework is steel rod, and the body is stuffed with trash salvaged from an old landfill where the bird once resided. When the landfill closed in 2000, the city rescued the sculpture and moved it to the present site.

Old and well-used athletic shoes compose the bird's pale underbelly. The top, neck, wings, and tail were composed of whatever else Olin S. Calk, the sculptor, could salvage. This includes discarded electric fans, used tires, computers, auto parts, sticks, stones, clothing, bicycle frames, raggedy tennis shoes, typewriter keyboards, and kitchen utensils. The beak was fashioned from tin buckets and sheet metal; the eyes were originally hubcaps; and the feet were constructed by wrapping wire around hunks of leather.

This majestic work may be viewed by taking the rest stop exit off Interstate 10 between mile markers 134 and 135, but it's only accessible to eastbound traffic.

Another oversized roadrunner perches along the road on the outskirts of Alamogordo, waiting for some metal critter to wander by so it can snarf it down for lunch.

Back in the 1990s, Basin Pipe and Metal needed something like a road sign to attract customers. At the same time, students in a local high school welding class needed a working project. A bargain was struck. The firm provided scrap metal and the students contributed the labor. The end result is a large roadrunner, skillfully crafted with smaller pieces of metal welded onto a steel frame to represent feathers, and larger sheets used for the tail and beak. This one stands about eight feet high and nearly fifteen feet long.

Ornithologists and amateur bird-watchers will find this giant beeper north of Alamogordo on US Highway 54, near where that road intersects with US Highway 82.

A Kid Named Billy

Lincoln County (and just about everywhere else)

Briefly, according to historical documents and extended research, this is what happened:

Henry McCarty was born in New York in either 1859 or 1860 to Catherine McCarty and a father whose name and fate have been lost in history. Mrs. McCarty and her two sons moved to Indianapolis, where she met William Antrim. They were married in Santa Fe and moved to Silver City, where Catherine died of tuberculosis. Young Henry's life of crime began shortly afterward when he was arrested

Although only one actual photograph of Billy the Kid is known to exist, his image appears on book covers, wanted posters, and historical documents.

but escaped from jail. The incident set the pattern for the remainder of his life.

He killed a man named Windy Cahill in Fort Grant, Arizona, on August 17, 1877, and was charged with "a criminal and unjustifiable shooting." He escaped prosecution and fled back to New Mexico where, over the years, he went under the name of William Bonney, Henry "Kid" Antrim, and El Chivato. He fought in the Lincoln County War, shot and killed at least three more men, became a legend, and was slain by Sheriff Pat Garrett on July 14, 1881.

End of story?

No way.

Since his death, Billy the Kid has entered the realm of immortality, sustained by a combination of myth, folklore, and legend, some of which occasionally includes some actual fact. He has been the subject of movies, novels, and scientific studies. He is honored in museums, has roads and stores named after him, and maintains a position of historical prominence more than 120 years later.

Much of his life story has been well documented, but here are Billy the Kid items of a nature so unusual that they deserve inclusion in any publication dealing with the curious:

- Billy has been the subject of more than sixty movies (the folks at the museum in Fort Sumner say it's more than 150 when foreign films are included).
- His grave site, located on an a rather isolated patch of ground adjacent to the Old Fort Sumner Museum, is surrounded by iron bars designed to keep tourists from tromping on his grave and stop them from stealing his grave stone. His remains lie between those of Tom O'Folliard and Charlie Bowdre, two of his saddle pals.
- The grave site is on Billy the Kid Road.
- The New Mexico Vacation Guide has a section entitled "Billy the Kid's Stomping Grounds."
- During a 2007 Billy the Kid exhibition in the Albuquerque Museum of Art and History, visitors were asked to vote on whether or not

Billy the Kid's grave site is surrounded by iron bars to make sure he finally stays put.

Billy should be pardoned, even now. The vote was more than two-to-one in his favor. The brochure for the exhibition noted that Billy loved to dance and his favorite tune was "Turkey in the Straw."

- Billy's image is preserved in tile and a wooden cutout at the Ruidoso Downs Visitor Center, and in a life-size wood carving in the entry of the Billy the Kid Museum in Fort Sumner. The museum also has one of those machines that smashes pennies into Billy the Kid souvenirs, along with sixty thousand Kid relics that include his rifle, chaps, spurs, and a variety of newspaper articles about men who claimed they were Billy, claimed they knew Billy personally, claimed they helped bury Billy, and claimed they helped Billy hide out after Pat Garrett's bullet missed him.

- People who don't get to see everything at the museum in one day can stay overnight at the Billy the Kid Country Inn, conveniently located just across the street.
- The Billy the Kid Scenic Byway starts at the Ruidoso Downs Visitor Center and wanders through Hondo, Lincoln, Fort Stanton, and Capitan before ending in Ruidoso.
- The only known photograph of Billy the Kid was a tintype take around 1880. Because tintypes presented a mirror image, this one created the mistaken belief that he was left-handed. In fact, Paul Newman even portrayed Billy as a portsider in the movie *Left-Handed Gun*.
- After Billy's death, the tintype was claimed by Dan Dedrick, an associate, who passed it down through his family. It eventually wound up in the hands of Dedrick descendants Stephen and Art Upham, who lent it to the Lincoln County Heritage Trust Museum for several years, then put it up for sale. Billionaire Bill Koch purchased it for $2.3 million during a 2011 auction in Denver.

One Way to Reduce Mayhem
Lordsburg

Shakespeare, a ghost town attraction on the edge of Lordsburg's city limits, was once a mining boomtown with a population of more than three thousand. But those days are gone and it's probably for the best, considering the town's rather colorful, but violent, history.

It was not a typical frontier town. It had twenty-three saloons but not a single church, newspaper, or school. Although located in an untamed, arid southwestern territory in the United States, it was named after a famous, and sophisticated, English writer. And the residents never elected a town marshal or city council because they dealt with lawbreakers in frontier fashion. For example, Russian Bill and Sandy King were both hanged in the dining room of the Butterfield Stage stop because there weren't any trees in town. Bill's crime was cheating on a mine claim; King got his for being "a darned nuisance."

Johnny Ringo, a contemporary of the men involved in the infamous gunfight at the OK Corral in Tombstone, Arizona, allegedly bought his last pair of boots here before his life was ended by a self-inflicted bullet wound to the head. And Beanbelly Smith made his niche in history when he shot and killed another man during an argument over who was going to get the last egg for breakfast in a local hotel.

Although it was unwritten, the locals did adhere to one rule: If you killed a man in Shakespeare, you had to bury him. The rule, coupled with the fact that the ground under and around the community was primarily rock, held the murder and "shot in self-defense" rate to a minimum.

When the silver boom ended, Shakespeare's population underwent a rapid decline. Worried about their investments, landowners and businessmen salted the nearby hills with low-grade diamonds in the hope that it would bring the fortune hunters back. It didn't work. By the early 1930s, everybody was gone. The property has been privately owned since 1935 and is open to the public only once or twice each month.

Shakespeare is two and a half miles southwest of Lordsburg off Main Street. Call (575) 542-9034 or visit shakespeareghostown.com for tour times and admission prices.

A Stone of Mystery

Los Lunas

The Mystery Rock is part of a basalt column that toppled over a long, long time ago in a valley below what is now called Hidden Mountain, about eighteen miles south of Los Lunas. What makes it a mystery are the 214 letters carved into its surface. They have been examined, re-examined, translated, photographed, studied, pored over, and deciphered for almost two hundred years, but nobody has come up with a definitive answer.

During all that research, the letters—and the words they form— were labeled Navajo, Mormon, Greek, Hebrew, Russian Cyrillic,

Etruscan, Egyptian, and, not infrequently, a hoax. Those who studied them came up with a variety of conclusions. One was that students from the University of New Mexico carved the letters as a prank. In another, a Harvard scientist proposed that the stone is a Hebrew Decalogue (the Ten Commandments). But others said it was a different version of the Ten Commandments, a conclusion that was hailed as the correct one until the 1970s, when an Albuquerque woman claimed it was written by Zakyneros, a Greek scholar who wrote in both ancient Phoenician and early Greek around 500 BC.

The actual age may never be firmly established because clean-up work at the site over the years has destroyed any possibility of using modern dating techniques. But one test that compared the inscription to that of a nearby petroglyph proclaimed the carvings are between five hundred and two thousand years old. Critics scoffed at that analysis, noting that the fifteen-hundred-year gap proved that the method of testing was inaccurate. The stone is easy to read today because Boy Scouts have regularly gone to the site and traced the letter outlines with chalk.

Linguists and thrill seekers who want to try their hands at answering the unanswered can still get to the rock but it's a difficult journey. It's located on land belonging to the Isleta Pueblo, so a permit from the State Land Grant Office in Albuquerque is an absolute necessity. Those who go there without a permit can be arrested and fined. Call the Land Grant Office at (505) 841-8705 for details.

Tanks for the Murals
Los Lunas (and Artesia and Truth or Consequences)

Water tank art isn't exactly common in New Mexico, but there's enough of it across the state to foster a sense of creativity. One of the best examples is in Los Lunas, where a huge city water tank is adorned with two snarling tigers.

There's a tiger on the east side and another on the west and all the space in between is filled with orange and black stripes, which is the

The Los Lunas High School Tigers show up on both sides of a city water storage tank.

way a tigered tank should look. The big felines were painted by Robert Vialpando, a local sign painter who has also served on the city council, to honor the athletes at Los Lunas High School because the school mascot is the tiger. The tank is very visible from Interstate 25 on the north edge of the city, about one half mile north of exit 203.

Artesia's huge water storage tank has been decorated to honor the Artesia High School Bulldogs and their dominance in football. A giant mural that encircles the tank depicts a mammoth bulldog surrounded by football helmets. Each helmet stands for a championship and the

★ ★

Bulldogs win one so often that the decor has been redone almost every other year.

Since 1957, the Bulldogs have won their division championship twenty-six times. That accumulation includes five "three-peats" (victories in three consecutive years) and a record of 454 wins against 148 losses and 15 ties. And, as another indication of the high regard accorded the grid squads, the town clock at the corner of South Seventh Street and West Main includes the Bulldogs' fight song in its chiming repertoire.

Just its name—Truth or Consequences—is enough to get Truth or Consequences into any curiosity publication, but its water tanks add more credibility to such a designation.

The Sierra County Arts Council commissioned Anthony Pennock to convert the city's two water tanks into works of art, and he performed the assigned task admirably, considering that his canvas was circular, made of steel, and more than thirty feet high. Pennock adorned them with Western scenes that reflect the area's heritage. The results are highly visible because water tanks, by their very nature, are usually placed on higher elevations and these are no exception to that rule of gravity. They look down on the city from its south side.

To Honor a Gridiron Great
Lovington

Brian Urlacher is big here, in more ways than one. He not only has a big reputation, but his countenance covers a billboard and the entire side of a downtown building. He is the local hero, the epitome of a hometown boy who made good. It's all because of his ability to play a game that has as its major component an air-filled ball made of animal skin.

Urlacher is a football player and a pretty darned good one. He became a star at Lovington High School, where he was named New Mexico's high school Player of the Year in 1995. Following graduation, he excelled at the University of New Mexico, where he was the Player

A Governor with a Grasp

While campaigning for governor of New Mexico on September 14, 2002, Bill Richardson attended two major events in Albuquerque. His primary purpose was to gather support to assist his run for the state's highest elected office, but he wound up becoming an entry in the Guinness World Records.

While working the crowds who attended the New Mexico University–Baylor football game in the afternoon and the New Mexico State Fair at night, Richardson was followed by a staff member armed with a counting device. Every time the candidate shook someone's hand, the staffer clicked the clicker.

By the end of the day, Richardson had shaken 13,392 outstretched hands, the most ever by any politician over an eight-hour period. The feat earned him a sore hand that had to be iced down, a spot in *Ripley's Believe It or Not!*, and the Guinness entry.

Apparently, it had the desired effect on the voters because seven weeks later, Richardson was elected in a landslide.

of the Year in the Mountain West Conference and was picked on three All-American teams.

The Chicago Bears selected Urlacher ninth in the National Football League's 2000 draft. Since then, he has been a mainstay at middle linebacker, has been named Defensive Rookie of the Year and Defensive Player of the Year, and has been invited to the Pro Bowl six times. Lovington honors its favorite son with the billboard bearing his photo and credentials on Highway 18 south of town, and a small

★ ★

Lovington's football hero Brian Urlacher is well-remembered in his hometown.

shrine in the Lovington Chamber of Commerce. And, of course, the twenty-foot tall face that covers the side of a building.

Although he no longer lives here, Urlacher comes back often to check on his automobile dealerships and to play in a charity basketball game.

Incidentally, sports analysts who frequently refer to outstanding football players as "animals" have a pretty good example in Urlacher. During his career, he has starred for the Lovington High School Wildcats, the University of New Mexico Lobos, and now the Chicago Bears.

★ ★

One Tough Castle
Montezuma

The castle sits on top of a hill so it has a good view of the surrounding territory, which always makes sense when building a fortress. But this castle was never meant to be a castle. It was a hotel, and a mighty fine one.

The Atchison, Topeka and Santa Fe Railroad built the opulent first Montezuma Hotel in 1887 as an exclusive resort for passengers who might be interested in moving to, or investing in, the West. Located in Montezuma just outside Las Vegas, the site was ideal because it offered natural hot springs, good fishing, and ample room for hiking and sightseeing. But two years after the grand opening, the hotel's gas lines plugged up and caused a fire that destroyed the building.

Undaunted, the railroad built a new hotel on the same spot, but this time it was the first building in New Mexico wired for electricity. It also burned down.

And still undaunted, the railroad went right back to work and erected a third hotel on the spot, only this time it was named the Phoenix Hotel because it, like the mythical bird, kept rising from its own ashes. But the locals still called it the Montezuma, and its days were also numbered. Unable to compete with the newer and less swanky resorts, the hotel closed its doors in 1904. After sitting vacant for several years, the building was converted into a seminary and served in that capacity for thirty years.

The Armand Hammer Foundation bought the property in 1981 and established the American campus of the United World College on the grounds. But the castle itself remained closed because it needed extensive repair, so the college used other buildings as classrooms and dormitories. Then, in 1997, the castle/hotel was placed on the list of America's 11 Most Endangered Historic Places and the following year, a White House council identified it as one of America's treasures. All that attention led to fundraising, followed by renovation. Now the castle has come full circle. Since 2002, it has served as living space for students and visitors.

Despite the name, Montezuma Castle has never been a castle.

And it is once again known as Montezuma Castle.

To get to the campus and the castle, take exit 343 off Interstate 25. Go one half mile and turn left onto New Mexico Avenue. Go 1.9 miles to the first traffic light, where you will turn left again onto Hot Springs Boulevard and continue a little over 4 miles, turning right when you see the castle. For more information, go to uwc-usa.org/tours or call (505) 454-4221.

There's Something in the Wind

Portales

Bill Dalley isn't sure why it happened, but he does remember the day he started collecting windmills. It was in the 1970s and he went to a friend's abandoned farmstead, looking for old lumber he could use in his woodworking shop. During the search, he found an old windmill, asked about it, and was told he could have it. So he dragged it home. "It just tickled my wife to death," he says with an impishly facetious grin, "but after a while, she got used to me bringing them home."

Now, almost thirty years after his first acquisition, Dalley's rural home is surrounded by windmills, and many of them still creak, spin, and groan in the wind. They're not all complete windmills, however. Some are sitting on their original steel and lumber stands; others are merely fans and blades. They range in size from standard to extra large, with some of the fans measuring up to eight feet across. Regardless of what shape they're in, he has almost ninety of them, collected from all across New Mexico and west Texas, and brought to his home in the back of a pickup truck.

It's still a hobby, Dalley says, not a windmilll museum. But curious passersby and serious windmill fanatics are always welcome to stop at his place and refresh their memories of the good old days when these wind-powered devices not only pumped water but also acted as grain-grinding mills.

Dalley's collection is on display day and night on his twenty-acre spread, located east of Portales two miles south of US Highway 70 on Kilgore Road. There's never a charge for stopping and looking, and on most days, Dalley will be on the grounds to conduct a personal tour, which is valuable because he knows each windmill personally and can usually relate at least part of its background.

★ ★

My, What Big Paws You Have
Raton

The road leading to Raton High School would look like any other strip of pavement that winds through a residential area up to an institution of learning except for the paw prints in one traffic lane. They're big and they're yellow, and they go for a couple of miles along the street, heading directly toward the school.

The reason for their existence is that the school's athletic teams are nicknamed the Tigers. The prints are placed on the streets by the Tiger Paws, a team support group composed primarily of athletes' fathers, who apply a new coat of paint to the markings every fall before football season begins.

The paws are not only an illustration of team spirit, but they also make it easy to find the school simply by following them. They're also meant to intimidate the teams who come to play the Tigers. They start at Tiger Drive, an extension of Clayton Road where it intersects with South Second Street.

To view them, take exit 451 off Interstate 25 and go west on Clayton Road. Go straight through the intersection with US Highway 64/Interstate 25 Business Loop onto Tiger Drive and follow it to the school.

Driving with Drumsticks
Red River

While most people stay at home on Thanksgiving, enjoying roasted turkey and all the stuff that goes with it, there are others who spend the day utilizing the bird in a completely different fashion: They ride frozen turkeys down a ski slope.

One of the winter events at the Red River Ski Area is the annual Turkey Toboggan, in which competitors careen down the snow-covered hills while seated on an unthawed turkey carcass. It's been going on for more than a decade, and up to forty bird racers compete every Thanksgiving. Usually, each contestant gets a couple of slides, which are timed to determine the winner. But sometimes the field gets so big that the racers get only one run down the beginners' slope.

Since frozen turkeys are rather difficult to steer, even when using the drumsticks as directional devices, spinouts and runaway carcasses are commonplace. The ski lodge furnishes the turkeys, which is undoubtedly a big relief to the Thanksgiving cooks who would rather prepare a fresh bird than one that's been sat upon.

For those who prefer something a little easier on the backside, the resort also offers cross-country skiing, Saturday night torchlight parades, and snowmobile rides to the top of 11,429-foot Greenie Peak. During the summer, when jockeying frozen turkeys and riding the flat slats down a mountain lose their popularity, Red River features drives along the Enchanted Circle Scenic Byway, wine festivals, chili cook-offs, and cross-town trolley excursions.

Daredevils looking for something more exciting than cranberry sauce and football games on Thanksgiving can get more information by logging on to redriverskiarea.com or by calling the lodge at (575) 754-2223.

The Curiosity Capital

Roswell

Any inquiry into weird stuff in New Mexico is commonly met with the same answer: "Roswell."

It's because of what occurred in the area on July 8, 1947. Briefly, a rancher came across the wreckage of what appeared to be an alien spacecraft. He reported it to authorities and the US Air Force issued a press release declaring that debris from a "crashed flying disc" had been recovered near the ranching community of Corona. After the international media storm that followed, the Air Force quickly retracted its original statement and said the wreckage was actually an experimental weather balloon. More than thirty years later, officials disclosed that it was part of a top-secret effort to monitor Soviet nuclear testing.

★ ★

But many still believe in a cover-up, that a UFO did crash, and that the federal government recovered an alien body near the crash site.

Regardless of which story, if any, is true, the city of Roswell has capitalized on the incident and taken up the UFO cause with substantial enthusiasm. There are reminders all over town. Some of the more notable include:

- The International UFO Museum and Research Center, located at 114 North Main Street, has greeted more than three million visitors since opening in 1992. An estimated 80 percent of those who visit Roswell for the first time say the museum was their primary reason for coming.

- The mailbox in front of the Roswell Visitor Center has been painted to resemble either a spaceship or R2-D2, the droid from the *Star Wars* movies.

The UFO Museum takes it all seriously and draws visitors by the millions, almost all of them earthlings.

**Little green men act as pitchmen in the
windows of Roswell souvenir shops.**

- The front of the local McDonald's is shaped like a flying saucer.
  Other alien-themed eateries include the Not of This World coffee-
  house, and the Cover Up Cafe. And Arby's has a sign out front that
  says WELCOME ALIENS.
- Coca-Cola machines in Roswell's downtown area feature green
  aliens drinking green Coke from a green bottle. Starchild, a gift
  and souvenir shop, displays white aliens and a spaceship above the

Clever use of metal slats has created
an alien face on a chain-link fence.

entryway. Roswell Landing, another souvenir dispensary, has an
alien-manned spaceship painted across the storefront.

- Gift shops sell T-shirts with such messages as "Aliens Rule" and
  "Aliens (the other gray meat). Gotta Love 'em. They taste just like
  chicken."

- The Wal-Mart logo on the building front incorporates an alien into
  its design, and many of the store's windows show aliens shopping
  for food, reading newspapers, and trying out fishing gear.

- The Roswell UFO Festival annually draws thousands of believers and
  skeptics, who discuss deep space and deep thinking with UFOlogists
  and sci-fi movie actors.

* The globes on streetlights along Main Street have been painted with slanty eyes so they resemble outer-spacers.

Need more convincing that Roswell has earned its reputation? Log on to roswellnm.org or call the museum at (800) 822-3545.

The message is clear, but a lot of human vehicles park there anyway.

★ ★

A Place to Get Hooked
Ruidoso

Antlers are a mainstay at Rustic Expressions, even though it's a furniture store and not a place that sells hunting supplies. This is because antlers are used in a variety of ways both to entice customers inside and then, once they're enticed, to convince them they need something antlerish.

The store's sign is the giveaway. It's made of countless sets of antlers—countless because they're intertwined, snarled, and all tangled together, making an accurate numerical assessment extremely difficult, if not impossible because antlers, by their very nature, do not line up in easily countable rows. They twist, turn, entangle, and otherwise make it difficult to determine exactly how many there are, especially when they're being used as a sign instead of performing more natural acts such as sitting on top of a deer's head or lying on the ground.

Inside the store, the selections include antler lamps, antler tables, and antler sculptures. And, as antler accents, the place also offers antler candle holders, antler bookends, and antler ash trays. But they don't sell antler chairs.

Those who need something different in an outdoorsy way will find Rustic Expressions at 1500 Sudderth Drive/Highway 48, phone number (575) 257-7743. Just walk right in; nobody's going to horn in on you. But be careful what you lean against.

A Boy Who Never Quite Grew Up
Sandia Park

Ross Ward started carving miniatures during his boyhood and was still creating them before his death in 1998. The result of that dedication to a dream is Tinkertown Museum, a fantasy land of little folks, the Old West, circus scenes, musicians, and other stuff, most of them carved from scrap lumber and all of them done to scale.

According to his autobiography, entitled *I Did All This While You Were Watching TV*, Ward's interest in small-scale things began after a visit to Knott's Berry Farm in California as a boy. He returned to his home in Aberdeen, South Dakota, and created a small town in his backyard. That one was leveled when the family moved, but Ward built others in between stints as a sign painter, circus hand, and Army draftee. In 1968, he and his wife bought a five-room cabin in the Sandia Mountains and gradually filled it with his carvings. They called the collection Tinkertown and took some of it on the road for a couple of years before converting the cabin into a museum that eventually grew into a twenty-four-room structure, each room filled with Ward's little people and little things.

Today, for a mere $3.50 or less, visitors can listen to animated musicians playing a folk tune, watch a circus parade, and examine the walls Ward created with fifty thousand empty bottles and tons of cement. They walk past old license plates used to cover uneven spots on the walls, step across horseshoes embedded in the concrete, and have their futures told by an automated Gypsy encased in an old fortune-telling device.

Since his death, Ward's family has taken over the operation, so they're in charge of thousands of carvings, musical instruments, animals, buildings, streets, and boardwalks, all created from scrap materials, all done while everyone else was watching television.

Tinkertown Museum is on the Turquoise Trail, at 121 Sandia Crest Road. For information and directions, visit tinkertown.com or call (505) 281-5233.

The Mysterious Staircase
Santa Fe

For more than a century, the staircase in the Loretto Chapel was considered a miracle. Or, at least, a work of unexplainably good carpentry.

The legend surrounding the stairs goes back to about 1873, when the Sisters of Loretto had a chapel built next to their school for girls. But the architect died before completing the plans and left no design for a staircase to get to the choir loft. The nuns appealed to local

★ ★

craftsmen but received no help, only suggestions that they use a ladder. So, according to the oft-told story, for nine days they prayed to St. Joseph, the carpenter. On the ninth day, according to the legend, a man showed up with a donkey and a toolbox and said he could handle the project.

He built a circular staircase that took up very little room and gave the nuns access to the loft, and he did it without using glue or nails. Then, the legend goes, he disappeared without asking for either payment or thanks, so the rumors began that it was St. Joseph himself who came to the rescue. Adding more mystery to the story was the theory that the wood used was impossible to find in the area.

As the legend grew, so did the crowds who came to see the miraculous staircase. But in the 1990s, skeptics started looking closely at the work, then set about debunking the story. Their investigations concluded that the stairs were built by a local Frenchman, Francois-Jean Rocha, and they produced records that indicate he bought the wood from a local lumberyard. Also, the doubters claimed, Rocha's obituary in the *Santa Fe New Mexican* in 1895 said he was the builder.

But the legend persists. And regardless of whether the popular story is fact or fiction, the staircase itself is a remarkable piece of woodworking. The chapel is now owned by the adjacent Inn at Loretto. The public can still view the staircase but there's an entry fee, payable at the front desk of the inn.

The chapel is located at 207 Old Santa Fe Trail in the downtown area. For more information, log on to lorettochapel.com or call (505) 982-0092.

A Double-Horned Bunny
Santa Fe

The world's largest jackalope sits in Douglas, Wyoming. It looks like a giant jackrabbit but it has antlers, it's made of fiberglass, and it guards the front entrance of the local fairgrounds. Douglas is a natural location for this attraction because the American jackalope's heritage can

A large blue jackalope attracts customers
to a Santa Fe commercial enterprise.

be directly traced to that city. Also, Wyoming trademarked the name in 1965 and even issues hunting licenses for the elusive creature.

But the world's largest *blue* jackalope stands silent watch in front of Jackalope, an import/export/antiques store located here. The creature is made of wood and spent most of its life hidden away in one of the store's back lots. But then it was resurrected, given a paint job, and placed in front of the establishment in the hope that it would draw customers, not scare them away. Mexican artist Alejandrino Fuentes gave the hybrid bunny its new look, accenting the basic blue with reds and whites.

The legend of the horned rabbits probably started in Europe in the 1600s, and then moved across the Atlantic. In the 1930s, Douglas taxidermist Doug Herrick conjured up a representation of the species by mounting the horns of small antelopes on the heads of jackrabbits. The creatures not only earned Herrick quite a bit of money, but also took on a life of their own. Jackalopes are now common inhabitants of gift shops and curio stores, and there are all sorts of jackalope rumors floating around, like the one that says they have developed vocal cords and often sing at night on the open prairie.

The big blue one is not for sale, but believers and nonbelievers alike can purchase jackalopes of all sizes in the store. There's even one that has a jackalope head mounted on the body of a chicken. It may or may not be the real thing.

The phone number at Jackalope is (505) 471-8539, but those who call shouldn't expect a jackalope to answer because it's beneath the creature's dignity to perform such menial tasks. After all, they're international icons.

The store is located at 2829 Cerrillos Road. For more information, log on to jackalope.com/location-santafe.html.

Burning Their Cares Away

Santa Fe

Every year in the first week of September, Santa Feans have an opportunity to watch their troubles go up in smoke, and they do this with considerable enthusiasm. As part of the annual Fiesta de Santa Fe, a huge marionette named Zozobra gets burned at the stake while thousands of onlookers cheer its fiery demise. It's because Zozobra is also known as Old Man Gloom, and his body is allegedly stuffed with all the trials, tribulations, woes, and travails of the previous year.

The fiesta has been held every year since 1712 to commemorate the retaking of the city from the Pueblo Indians. But Zozobra didn't become part of the celebration until 1924, when artist Will Shuster built the first one and invited some friends to his home, where they theoretically disposed of their troubles by turning them into ashes. Shuster based his creation on a Yaqui Indian custom of burning an effigy of Judas during Holy Week. He turned all rights to Zozobra over to the local Kiwanis Club in 1964, and that organization has not only continued the tradition, but also used it to earn more than three hundred thousand dollars for student scholarships.

Because Zozobra is destroyed every year, a new one has to be made the next year. The figure stands about fifty feet tall and is made of precut wooden strips covered with chicken wire and muslin, then painted. The body is stuffed with shredded paper—usually things like police reports, divorce papers, and paid-off mortgages. The creation process takes up to three weeks and involves about three thousand volunteer hours.

Once in place, in front of as many as forty thousand cheering onlookers, Zozobra begins waving its arms and uttering ferocious growls as the flames surround it, destroying all the cares and troubles of the past. Even last-minute attendees are invited to include their worries. A gloom box is placed near the band stage, and all articles placed inside are added to the pyre.

Newspaper ads herald the annual
immolation of Zozobra in Santa Fe.

The festivities begin at dusk in Fort Marcy Park, and require admission tickets. There's no parking near the site, but park and ride options are available at local malls and bus terminals. The event has also spawned a line of merchandise. Items include T-shirts, stickers, shot glasses, temporary tattoos, pins, earrings, ball caps, beanies, and DVDs, all available at a Zozobra booth on the downtown plaza in the days before and after the immolation.

Amateur pyromaniacs who need more information can find it by checking out kiwanis-sf.org/zozobra.aspx.

Go Ahead; We're Listening
Socorro County

When driving along US Highway 60 west of Socorro, motorists encounter a series of huge white things that look like giant television receptors suddenly looming on the horizon. They are known as the

**The Very Large Array has been listening to
outer space for more than 25 years.**

Very Large Array, part of the National Radio Astronomy Observatory's huge composite radio telescope that listens for and captures radio waves from outer space.

The array consists of twenty-seven dish-shaped antennas, each measuring eighty-two feet across and weighing 230 tons. They are arranged in a Y-shaped configuration on tracks along a trio of thirteen-mile stretches on the Plains of San Agustin. The data from the dishes is combined electronically to give the resolution of an antenna twenty-two miles across.

Since its inception, the VLA has made more scientific discoveries than any other ground-based telescope in the history of such research. The giant platters have also starred in the Jodie Foster movie *Contact* and several documentaries. But they still haven't heard from anyone trying to relocate from Mars.

★ ★

The VLA visitor center is open daily and guided tours are conducted twice per year. Self-guided walking tours can be taken from 8:30 to dusk. To get there, take US Highway 60 west of Socorro for sixty-two miles, then turn south on Highway 52 for two miles to the access road. For details, log on to vla.nrao.edu or contact the education office at (507) 835-7243.

Keeping an Eye on the Food
Taos

Eating a meal at the Kiva Coffee Shop can be a bit unnerving if you feel uncomfortable when there's somebody watching each spoonful as you launch it stomachward.

The dining spot, located in the Best Western Kachina Lodge, was built by Edwin Lineberry, who patterned it after the kivas found in many of the Native American pueblos and villages in New Mexico and Arizona. So it's round, and the ceiling is held up by a series of *vigas* (log poles) that extend like spokes from a center column to the edges.

It's that center column that catches the eye, in a very real sense. It's a totem pole, designed and carved by artist Duane VanVechten, Lineberry's wife. It's very big and it sits in the middle of a circular counter and the eyes look right down into your bacon and eggs. Since the eyes are in proportion to the totem, they're also very big, so they create an impression that you'd better watch your manners because there's something monster-sized keeping an eye on you.

The lodge and coffee shop, at 413 Paseo del Pueblo Norte, can be reached by following US Highway 64 through town. The lodge is on the east side of the road between Brook Street and Montecito Lane. For reservations or more information, visit kachinalodge.com/node/71 or call (800) 522-4462.

Giant totem pole in a Taos restaurant

★ ★

Saving the Planet Bottle by Bottle
Taos

When the people in charge of construction at Earthship need building materials, they don't go to a lumberyard or hardware store for two-by-fours, reinforcing rods, or drywall. Instead, they acquire items commonly found in dump grounds (now politically correctly referred to as "sanitary landfills").

So when the building project begins, the workers use discarded bottles, treadless tires, once-used metal cans, concrete, and a lot of

Old tires and beer bottles are construction material at Earthship.

dirt to convert throwaways into homes that they hope will help save the world. The buildings are self-sufficient, low-impact structures that rely heavily on recycling and nature. They harvest and recycle rain and groundwater, have their own contained sewage treatment operations, use solar and thermal power for heating and cooling, and get electric power from the sun and wind. The concept, known as Earthship Biotecture, originated here and has spread across the world.

The Greater World Earthship Community here is composed of a visitor center, permanent homes, and rental properties on 660 acres, with 347 acres set aside as commonly owned open space. One of the rentals is the Phoenix Studio and Suite, a more advanced form of planet-saving housing. It contains 5,400 square feet and has three bedrooms, two bathrooms, and Wi-Fi Internet access. The entire house sleeps six, but small groups can stay in either the East Wing (sleeps four) or West Wing (sleeps two).

Architects, futurists, and plain old curious folks can get there by taking US Highway 64 west from Taos across the Rio Grande Gorge Bridge and following the signs for another one and a half miles to the center on the right. There's a fee for roaming around the grounds on self-guided tours. For information, visit earthship.com or call (575) 751-0462.

A Rock Ship of the Desert
Tesuque

Most of the time, you have to squint, stand in exactly the right spot, and/or use a lot of imagination to see the figure, shape, or face that's supposed to be represented in a rock formation. And then it usually doesn't look like what it's supposed to look like.

But not Camel Rock.

It's a big chunk of eroded sandstone that looks just like a camel, no matter how you view it. It has a hump, long neck, big nose, and, when the sun's just right, flaring nostrils, just like those real ships of the desert that hang around the pyramids, Russian circus rings, and

zoos across America. Besides that, you don't have to hike across can-
yons and scramble down into gulches to see this creature of stone
because it's about forty feet high, and it's sitting right next to a major
roadway north of Santa Fe.

Even better, you can drive your car right up to it because some
wise person designated the area as Camel Rock Monument. So there's
plenty of parking right next to a stone walkway that leads directly to
the beast. Getting there is easy: Take exit 175 off US Highway 285.
You can't miss it. And you'll know you're in the right area because
several nearby businesses and a casino have incorporated Camel Rock
into their names.

4

West Texas

Texas is big. *The* Texas Almanac *says it's 268,581 square miles. Wikipedia says it's 268,820 square miles and the US Census Bureau lists it at 261,797 square miles. That's a lot of acreage, so there's plenty of room for weird stuff.*

And there's no dispute over weird stuff in Texas. Over the years, and across the miles, authors John Kelso and Sharry Buckner have come across such curiosities as a gigantic concrete structure that originally stored oil but later was used as a trout farm, a cheating scandal in a major chili cook-off, a bogus story about watching a football game in a local saloon that still riles some Texans, and Stanley Marsh 3, who is so unusual that he almost deserves an entire chapter all to himself.

Within its boundaries, Texans lay claim to such weirdness as a free steak if your belly can hold seventy-two ounces of meat and taters, bans on public dancing, an artist who uses junked auto parts to create dinosaurs, and a ninety-foot steel cross standing in the middle of the flatlands.

Twenty Texans once stripped to their birthday suits because they thought the devil was in their clothing. They hit a tree and had to stand around naked while police investigated. Other Texans eat goat testicles and claim they taste pretty good. A Texan created a version of Stonehenge on his ranch. Another Texan collects toasters.

See? Texas is weird.

And this book contains only weirdness from West Texas and the panhandle. Think of what else is out there in other parts of the state, waiting to elevate your curiosity levels to their highest degree.

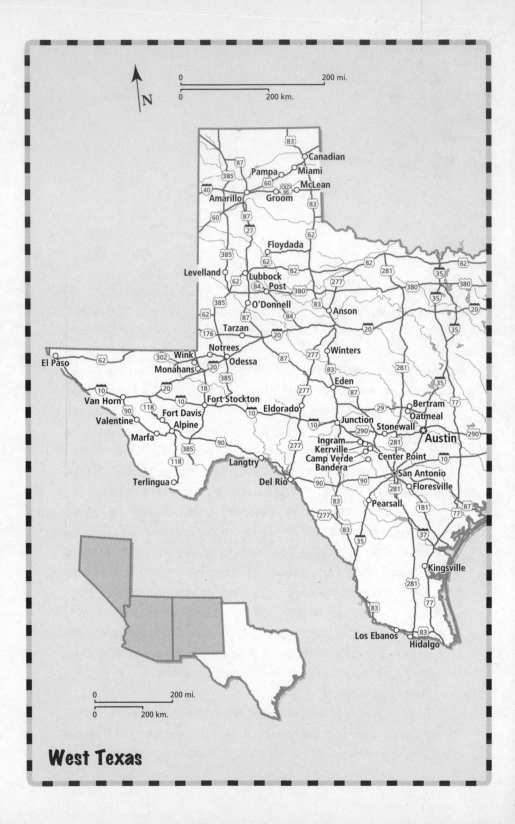

West Texas

Jackassic Park

Alpine

You'll see the billboards for the Apache Trading Post before you see the blue log cabin on US Highway 90 at the western edge of town. Inside, you'll find an amazing gift shop and art gallery, but outside you'll find Jackassic Park.

Home of cute mules and burros, this is a great photo op—if you like those silly cutout boards you stick your head through and grin at the camera. Have your picture taken with the asses or as an ass.

Have your picture taken as "Smart-Ass," "Dumb-Ass," "Candy-Ass," "Lazy-Ass," or "½-Ass."
AL BUCKNER

★ ★

Choose to be "Smart Ass," "Dumb Ass," "Candy Ass," "Lazy Ass," or "½-Ass." If you have four friends along, you can be all five.

For information on this cultural experience, located at 2701 West Highway 90, call (432) 837-5506, or log on to apachetradingpost.com.

The Dynamite Museum
Amarillo

There are three reasons why there's no address listed for the Dynamite Museum. First, it's not a museum. Second, it has nothing to do with dynamite. Third, it doesn't have an address.

It was another spacey art project from Amarillo's Stanley Marsh 3, heir to an oil and gas fortune, who owned KVII-TV here and has a taxi-dermied hog on the floor of his cluttered office in the Bank One Tower.

The Dynamite Museum was an art-sign project that involved Marsh and a bunch of college students he recruited going all over town on Saturdays putting signs in people's yards. The signs are the same size and shape as highway warning signs, but instead of saying ROAD WORK AHEAD or SLOW TO 60, they have messages such as I HAVE TRICKS UP MY SLEEVE, I FOUND A BLUE SPIDER IN THE CORNER AND KILLED HIM WITH A BROOM, I'LL DO AS I PLEASE, BIG ROCK CANDY MOUNTAIN, and YOU'RE WITH THE BAD BOYS NOW, BABY. They got the sayings from a variety of sources, including books, novels, deejays, Hank Williams, and Shakespeare.

Marsh no longer works on that project. "I got tired of it," he said, "but I might do it again sometime." Still, thousands of the signs are scattered all over Amarillo and the Panhandle. "People move them when they move," Marsh said. He claims he saw one that had been converted into a basketball goal.

He said most of the kids who helped him make and distribute the signs were creative types. "I don't think I recruited anybody who didn't want to be a rock star or a famous author," he said. "We never recruited anybody practical who wanted to learn about cement."

You knew these pranksters when you saw them. They traveled in a caravan of vehicles that included a 1959 pink Cadillac; a flatbed truck with a buffalo head on the back, hauled by a van with a merry-go-round horse on the roof; a van completely covered with GOD BLESS JOHN WAYNE bumper stickers; and another van with a couple of yard geese riding on top.

The project began after Marsh saw signs near a railroad crossing that he thought were depressing. One of them read ROAD ENDS 300 FEET. So he put up his own sign: ROAD DOES NOT END.

Marsh also bankrolled Cadillac Ranch, another funky work of art located in a cow pasture next to Interstate 40 near Amarillo. Ten Cadillacs are buried nose down in the ground with their tail fins thrust toward the sky. Established to outline the history of changes to the Cadillac tail fin, the display is the Panhandle's answer to the Statue of Liberty. It's what you go to look at when you're up this way.

Despite its unorthodox nature and questionability as art, it's next to impossible to drive by when there's nobody there. Tourists from all over the world have put it on their "must see" lists.

In 1998, the Caddies were decorated for the holiday season. They were painted like Christmas trees—green, with tinsel and ornaments and all sorts of other Yuletide decorations. In January 2012, a group of campaigners painted all the cars to show support for Ron Paul's presidential bid.

Lightnin' McDuff

Amarillo

This sculptor makes a living making art out of junk. "The majority of 'em are one hundred percent recycled, or close to it," said Lightnin' McDuff, a slow-talking, pony-tailed, lanky drink of water. "These deer—the legs are made out of new steel, but the bodies and the heads are old farm discs, and the antlers are pitchfork tines."

McDuff, who gets his inspiration from reading and visiting junkyards, pointed out his prices are less than many other sculptors' because "what you're buying here is my imagination and my work,

★ ★

instead of expensive material. I go to scrap iron yards, garage sales, and farm auctions. Every once in a while, some farmer will call and say, 'I've got a bunch of stuff out behind here, why don't you come by and haul some of it off?' And I do."

The stuff becomes art and gets a price tag. His works run two hundred dollars and up. His most popular works, he said, are his deer and buffalo. "I was raised working with livestock as a kid growing up," he explained, "so you'll find a lot of critters here. And the thing is, I don't have to feed and water 'em every day." The buffalo that used to decorate his studio was made out of the ends of propane tanks, along with some steel rod for eyebrows.

Perhaps his best work was his pet, the Maniac Mutt, a nasty-looking junkyard dog made out of scraps from other art projects. Lightnin' kept the Maniac Mutt chained in the back of his truck. "A fella with a gimme hat on his head and a flatbed truck needs a bad dog in this part of the world," he said. "I had to keep him chained 'cause he likes to jump out and eat the hubcaps off Mercedes. That's his favorite snack."

The bad news is that Maniac Mutt is no longer in the back of the truck because he got sold to a guy in Arizona. The good news is that Lightnin' has built several other similar mutts since then, although he said people keep snapping them up. So he remains muttless.

Lightnin's art, and his truck, are usually at 508 South Bowie. His phone number is (806) 376-5045.

The Big Texan Steak Ranch
Amarillo

If you've ever had a hankering to consume a piece of meat the size of a double-wide, the Big Texan Steak Ranch is the restaurant for you.

If you can finish off the seventy-two-ounce top sirloin in an hour or less, it's yours for free—if you can also down the baked potato, shrimp cocktail, dinner roll, and salad that come with it. If not, it'll cost you more than $72.

★ ★

So what is it that gets them? "It's the croutons," joked Bobby Lee, one of the owners. Since 1962, when the challenge began (at a price of $9.95), more than 61,000 people have tried to complete the meal, and about 8,600 of them have been successful. The others suffered from gas. "It's about the size of a catcher's mitt," Lee said when describing the chunk of cow meat placed in front of the challengers.

Not everyone who has accomplished the task has been a hulk. Lee said a 120-pound reporter from the *Wall Street Journal* ate the whole thing. But he didn't say if that weight was before or after. In the summer of 2009, a seventy-year-old man displaced the reigning champion, a sixty-nine-year-old grandmother, as the oldest person to eat the whole thing. The youngest was an eleven-year-old boy who asked for dessert afterward.

Former Cincinnati Reds pitcher Frank Pastore, who has eaten the whole thing seven times, set a fastest-time record of 9.5 minutes in 1987, and the mark stood until 2008, when Joey "Jaws" Chestnut snarfed down the entire meal in 8 minutes, 52 seconds. Chestnut is an internationally known eating champion and holds a variety of fast-gobbling records.

The unofficial record belongs to a five-hundred-pound Bengal tiger owned by Benjamin Heiple of Florida. His meal was limited to the steak only and his technique was simple—sniff, lick, gulp. It took him less than ninety seconds.

Every once in a while, someone will make practical use of the steak deal. One customer ordered it, then ignored the one-hour limit and took his sweet time eating. Then he ordered a dozen extra rolls and told the staff he was headed to California and wanted to make some sandwiches.

It hasn't been all fun and games at the Big Texan Steak Ranch, though. In 1998, an escaped convict from Indiana shot himself to death in the restaurant's adjoining motel after police came and surrounded the place. Ever since, Lee maintains, there has been "weird stuff going on in that room."

★ ★

To get this steak for free, you have to finish it in an hour or less.
JOHN KELSO

And in October 2003, George, the restaurant's pet rattler, got loose from his cage in the gift shop. This presented a thrill for the management, because the restaurant was open at the time and they really didn't want George crawling up some tourist's leg. "We found it in about twenty minutes," Lee said. "That was the longest twenty minutes of my life." George's run to freedom was brief—and deadly. After his recapture, the ramblin' rattler was put down.

The Big Texan Steak Ranch is located off Interstate 40's exit 75. For more information on how to get rid of them thar hunger pangs, log on to bigtexan.com or call (806) 372-6000.

Poetry in Motion

Near Amarillo

For those in the mood to be put on, this concrete parody of Percy Bysshe Shelley's poem "Ozymandias" is something they can't afford to miss.

The poem reads, in part:

I met a traveler from an antique land
Who said: "Two vast and trunkless legs of stone
Stand in the desert."

In an obvious effort to tweak everybody's nose, Stanley Marsh 3 (he of the Dynamite Museum and Cadillac Ranch fame) teamed up with Lightnin' McDuff (who sculpts deer figures out of old farm discs) to build two large, trunkless legs. However, these are made of concrete reinforced with steel, not stone. But they are vast—one stands twenty-four feet high and the other thirty-four feet tall.

The legs get a lot of attention. "People go there sometimes and paint the toenails," Marsh said. "And I understand there have been three marriages out there."

The legs may not be standing in the desert, exactly, but they are standing behind a barbed-wire fence all by themselves in a pasture off Interstate 27 at Sundown Lane, south of Amarillo. You can't miss them. They're the only big concrete legs with large feet out there.

The work, like the poem, is called *Ozymandias*. Why did Marsh pick this particular work? "It's a poem about the futility of building monuments so, of course, I built a monument to it," he explained.

The legs come with a phony Texas historical marker Marsh concocted to further muddy the waters. The marker says that Shelley penned his poem at this location in 1819 when he and his wife, Mary Wollstonecraft Shelley, the author of *Frankenstein*, discovered these ruins while "on their horseback trek over the great plains of New Spain."

Almost everything on the marker is complete and utter horse doots, including the paragraph at the bottom that explains why the legs have

If you build it, they will come.
JOHN KELSO

no face: "The visage (or face) was damaged by students from Lubbock after losing to Amarillo in competition." The marker says the face will be replaced, and if you want to see the original, you can find it at the Amarillo Museum of Natural History,

There is no Amarillo Museum of Natural History. But Marsh said people inquire all the time, trying to find it.

Incidentally, after unknown pranksters painted gym socks on the legs, Marsh claimed he didn't do it, but since he liked it, he took credit for it.

So Many John Waynes, So Little Time
Bandera

If you don't like looking at John Wayne, stay out of the Old Spanish Trail Restaurant here. The walls of the back dining room are lined with hundreds of paintings and photos of America's favorite red-blooded Western guy.

You've got John Wayne in an Army uniform from his role in *The Green Berets* (even though he never served in the military), John Wayne as Davy Crockett in a coonskin cap from *The Alamo*, and John Wayne as a multitude of other fighting men.

"He's just always been like a hero of mine, and I always thought that Bandera was perfect for that room," said Gwen Janes, who bought the restaurant in 1978.

People continuously add to the collection. For example, a huge canvas of Wayne was donated by a man in Florida because his wife hated the thing. But John Wayne himself never made it to the Old Spanish Restaurant. Janes has always resisted customer suggestions that she tell people he once ate here, saying she wasn't about to lie about it because John Wayne wouldn't have lied about it, either.

If you don't get enough of John Wayne from the wall hangings, they keep a DVD player in the John Wayne Room and play John Wayne movies on it. The restaurant is at 305 Main Street. For directions and details, call (830) 796-3836.

No Dancin' in Anson

The trouble with dancing is that it could lead to hanky panky. Hence, the ban on dancing on campus at Baylor University in Waco. That prohibition finally came to an end after 151 years with a street dance on April 19, 1996.

But Baylor wasn't the only place in Texas that stomped out dancing over the years. Until 1987, when a group of parents called the Footloose Club challenged the fifty-four-year-old law that banned public dances, there was no dancin' in the West Texas town of Anson. "No Dancin' in Anson" became an oft-used headline around the world. The Footloose Club parents wanted their children to be able to have their own prom. The fight got pretty ugly, with a Baptist preacher declaring that girls could get pregnant on the dance floor.

Hey, girls could get pregnant at the Laundromat, but that doesn't mean you should stop washing your clothes.

You're probably wondering at this point if the Anson ordinance was ever enforced. You bet your ballet slippers it was.

"I know at least one year the chief closed down a proposed prom," said Ricardo Ainslie, educational psychology professor at the University of Texas and the author of *No Dancin' in Anson: An American Story of Race and Social Change*. Ainslie said the chief of police showed up at the mid-1980s prom before dancing could break out. So the prom was moved to a Catholic church outside the city limits.

The Anson ordinance, passed in 1933, made dancing a five- to fifteen-dollar fine, quite a chunk of change during the Depression. The ordinance was written in such a way that you could get busted for dancing more than once in the same day. So if you were caught dancing two or three times in the same day, it could have gotten pretty expensive.

Decapitated Chicken Car
Bandera

The excitement began with theft on New Year's Eve, 2008. Whether or not the burglar knew it, he'd stolen an icon—the giant rooster head perched atop the 1977 Cadillac known all around southwest Texas as "the chicken car from Bandera."

The car sports a five-foot fiberglass head with blinking eyes and an electronic "cackle" and also has a rooster tail affixed to the rear. It's usually parked in front of Church's Fried Chicken on Main Street. Some theorized the theft was a prank. Or maybe a monster chicken

The famous chickmobile of Bandera
AL BUCKNER

247

hawk had done the deed. But Janice Bowen, the franchise owner who helped create the chicken car in 1994, wasn't amused. She offered a five-hundred-dollar reward for the pilfered poultry.

Nearly a month later, the missing head was spotted near a dumpster in Kerrville and returned. And once again, all parades in Bandera feature their fowl participant rolling along to the strains of—what else?—the "Chicken Dance."

Dinosaur Made from Junked Parts
Bertram

The head is two oil pans rigged up to a windshield-wiper motor. Turn it on and the dinosaur's jaw flaps. The teeth are spark plugs, the toes are off a farm cultivator, and the vertebrae welded in the neck are rocker arms for motor valves.

The late Garrett Wilkinson, a welder, created two junk dinosaurs during his lifetime. He built the first one after Bertram city officials asked him to make a beast to go along with the discovery of some dinosaur tracks in the creek at nearby Oatmeal. They said they hoped it would bring in tourists. Wilkinson said he didn't know how to make dinosaur skin, but he said he could rig up a skeleton.

The second dinosaur was built because of popular demand, after he sold the first one to a man from San Angelo. After many people drove by the site and wondered where the prehistoric assortment of junked parts had gone, Wilkinson decided to create a second giant. It can still be seen in Bertram, parked on TX 29 as you come into town from the east, or outside Wilkinson's old welding shop on Vaughn Street. The dino is real easy to spot during the Christmas season because family members put lights on him, plug them in, and light him up.

During his lifetime, Wilkinson created more than one hundred whimsical metal sculptures, many of which can still be seen around the city.

Back by popular demand
JOHN KELSO

It's a Bird, It's a Plane, It's a Camel
Camp Verde

Camp Verde, the Army post on the banks of the Verde Creek, is probably most famous for the great "camel experiment." In 1854, US Secretary of War Jefferson Davis had a bright idea to use camels for supply transports in the dry southwest. Congress appropriated the money, and the first shipment of thirty-three camels and four drivers arrived from Egypt in 1856.

★ ★

A reminder of the past at Camp Verde
AL BUCKNER

During the Civil War, the camp was captured by Confederate forces; when the war ended and the fort was recaptured, the size of the herd had increased to more than one hundred camels. So the experiment was declared a success. Temporarily, at least. The camels could carry heavier loads and travel longer distances than horses or mules, but the War Department ended the experiment and deactivated the fort in 1869.

★ ★

There are several versions of what happened next. Camels were sold to zoos and circuses, and men tried to use them to haul various items to various places. Stories that they were let loose, turned wild, and terrified area inhabitants were common, but generally disbelieved.

All that remains today is the restored general store, originally built in 1857 to provide the soldiers with supplies, mostly liquor. Today, it's an upscale gift shop and cafe featuring oodles of camel memorabilia and an abstract steel sculpture of a beast of burden. The store is at 285 Camp Verde Road East.

For more information, log on to campverdegeneralstore.com or call (830) 634-7722.

Concrete Yard Collection
Canadian

Bobby Gene "Pig" Cockrell's well-endowed concrete Dallas Cowboys cheerleader didn't stay naked long. These days she's got on hot pants, a tank top, and boots.

"My neighbor and my wife put some clothes on her," Cockrell said. "They didn't think that would look too nice out in the front yard."

But what did Pig think of her? "It looked pretty good to me," he said.

Most of the concrete items Cockrell makes and puts in his yard aren't risqué. There are twenty-six sculptures in all. His favorite is the cowboy outhouse scene. You see the wooden outhouse and the reins from the horse leading into the outhouse. But you don't see the cowboy. "It looks just like the cowboy rode up to the outhouse and run in and held the reins so his horse wouldn't run off," the artist explained.

He's also got a buffalo, a two-headed dragon, and a concrete family from outer space. "I got three aliens—a mama, a papa, a baby, and an alien dog. And I've got a flying saucer on top of it," he said.

Pig began making concrete yard art in the mid-1990s. So what got him started? "Oh, I dunno," he answered. "I couldn't fish and hunt at the time, so I had to do something else."

Canadian, a community of slightly under twenty-five hundred, is the seat of Hemphill County and home of the Happy State Bank. It's named after the Canadian River, a tributary of the nearby Arkansas River, and is known as "the oasis of the Texas Panhandle." Portions of the Tom Hanks film *Castaway* were filmed here.

If He Had a Hammer . . .
Center Point

Butch Lackey has hammers—more than two thousand of them at last count. He also has literally thousands of saws, wrenches, screwdrivers, hatchets, drills, scythes, shovels, rakes, and pitchforks. And other assorted tools and farm implements.

His collections fill four buildings behind his home, which he shares with his lovely, indulgent wife, Betty. Actually, his collections more

Hammers and more hammers at Butch Lackey's place
AL BUCKNER

than just fill the buildings; they cover the walls and hang from the ceilings.

He has painted some tools with vibrant colors and artfully arranged others, like his screwdriver displays, which radiate out in graceful circles.

How did all this start? Well, about thirty years ago, Lackey found a toolbox that contained at least ten hammers. He said he picked it up, put it in his truck, and wondered, as he drove home, what he could do with all those hammers.

Obviously, he came up with a plan.

The Brinkley Mansion
Del Rio

You might want to call this place a quack house. That's because the man who built it, Dr. John Brinkley, was perhaps the most colorful and successful quack in the history of the United States.

Brinkley invented the so-called goat gland operation. During his bizarre and checkered career, it was estimated he performed the surgery on more than sixteen thousand men. For $750, Brinkley would take the testicle from a Toggenburg goat, slice it up, then insert a sliver into his patient in an operation that would allegedly cure prostate problems and enhance the patient's sexual performance.

Brinkley started the goat gland surgeries in the late 1920s, about the time he moved to the small border town of Del Rio. By the late 1930s, he had advanced his technique to a more sophisticated injection of fluid. He also sold a line of patent medicines—Nos. 1 through 45, each supposedly designed to cure a different ailment.

Brinkley moved to Del Rio so he could build himself a radio station with an extremely powerful signal out of Mexico. The office of XER (the station's call letters) was in Del Rio, but the transmitter was across the Rio Grande in Via Acuna, where it couldn't be regulated by the US government. In the 1930s, Brinkley would go on the air, talk about religion and politics, sell pieces of wood that he claimed were from the cross of Jesus Christ, and push his medicine. He also was depositing three thousand dollars a day in the bank just from the sale of his little one-dollar paperback book entitled *Dr. Brinkley's Doctor Book*.

On the air, Brinkley would invite his listeners to come see the show of an evening at the Brinkley House on Qualia Drive, with the two "Dancing Waters" fountains in the front. People would gather in the five-acre park across the street. The water, colored with lights, would shoot forty feet into the air, go into a mist pattern, and perform other tricks to the sound of Brinkley's 1,063-pipe organ. For the amusement of onlookers, Brinkley's exotic animals—penguins, rare giant Galapagos tortoises, and flamingos—would be released from their pens to roam the grounds.

At one point, to gain accreditation, Brinkley visited Benito Mussolini, the Italian dictator, who got him an honorary degree from a medical school in Rome.

But it all began to crumble in the late 1930s. People began suing Brinkley, who tried to dodge the inevitable by dividing up the estate among his family members, including his wife, Minnie Telitha Brinkley, and son John "Johnny Boy" Richard Brinkley III. The elder Brinkley died in 1943. By the early 1970s, attorneys suing the family had chewed up all the money. Distraught, Johnny Boy killed himself.

The mansion, at 512 Qualia Drive, had been designated a Texas Historic Landmark but is now privately owned and not open to the public. But you can still drive by and look.

Beer Joint? What Beer Joint?

Eden

Long before Jayson Blair and the scandal at the *New York Times*, a former writer for the *Chicago Sun-Times* named Wade Roberts allegedly came to this small West Texas town and did a feature story on a Dallas Cowboys–Chicago Bears football game from a local bar called Bonner's. Trouble was that at that time, mid-November 1985, there was no beer joint in Eden called Bonner's. In fact, there was no beer

Fact? Fiction? Or just too much beer?
JOHN KELSO

joint in Eden at all—and there still isn't—according to Kathy Amos, publisher and editor of the *Eden Echo*, who is still chapped about the scam.

"Only when people like you bring it up again is it remembered," said Kathy, who has been the newspaper editor here since 1978. "Otherwise, we blissfully let time erase it. It's just maddening when somebody pulls a scam on you, whether it's a harmless thing or a bad thing. You feel kind of helpless."

It may not have been a true story, but it was very well written. Good ol' boys had gathered in this Bonner's bar that had pickled eggs to watch the Bears kick the snot out of the Cowboys, 44-0. The owner of the place was named Jefferson Davis Bonner. (You can't make this

★ ☆ ★ ☆ ★ ☆ ★ ☆ ★ ☆ ★ ☆ ★ ☆ ★ ☆ ★ ☆ ★ ☆ ★ ☆ ★ ☆ ★ ☆ ★ ☆ ★ ☆ ★ ☆ ★

kind of stuff up. Wait. Yes you can.) There was a guy in the bar named Les Smalley, "a craggy weathered rancher known as Buster."

The story has it that as the boys gathered around the bar's TV set, they tried to enlist Smalley in a bet:

"'Sorry,' said Smalley, looking timid all of a sudden. 'Done made my bet today.'"

"'Just who and what,' demanded Bonner, 'are you bettin'?'"

"'The wife. The Cowboys win, and she don't bother me the rest of the season. The Bears win, and I don't get no football 'til the Super Bowl.'"

Toward the end of the story, the distraught Smalley is described with "his lower lip hanging lower than his Mack truck belt buckle." Then there's the perfect finale when somebody punches E7 on the jukebox, and they all accompany Bobby Bare in a round of "Drop Kick Me Jesus (Through the Goalposts of Life)."

There was no jukebox. In fact, after the article came out, Roberts came to Eden and spent two days with his boss trying to find Bonner's so he could clear himself. No such luck. The newspaper asked Roberts to split.

Amos didn't remember the writer's name, but she put it this way: "It was somebody who didn't want to work that weekend or something. Nothing like that existed here. A restaurant or two serves beer, but there was not your basic beer joint, no."

Pity. The story read so well it made me want to eat a pickled egg and take the Cowboys and the points.

On Your Mark. Get Set. Goat!
Eldorado

Much of the talk around here the last several years has been about the polygamy compound that sprang up in 2003 north of town.

"Oh, man, that's somethin', isn't it? We don't know what to think of 'em," said Jim Runge, a local character who inadvertently diverts attention from the multiple-wives situation by putting on the Elgoatarod, an April Fools Day weekend goat-oriented celebration.

★ ★

The central event of the Elgoatarod—a takeoff of the Iditarod, the 1,170-mile cross-country Alaskan dogsled race—is a series of four goat races held around the courthouse square. Goats pull "sled knockoffs" about two hundred yards and among the sleds, Runge said, "one is a chariot, one is a galactic goat—it's like a spaceship—one is like a covered wagon. We've had 'em bring along inverted dollies and little red wagons and a converted riding lawn mower with everything taken off but its wheels."

Along with a parade, the event features a goat-pill-flipping contest, a chigger-catching contest, gnat races, and a goat-fry cook-off. Goat fries are fried goat testicles.

There's also an ugliest goat contest. "Ugliest goat wins, but it has to be a goat," Runge said. "Cain't be a human. A wife brought her husband and said, 'He's an old goat,' but it has to be a goat. Cain't be a husband."

The Fundamentalist Church of Jesus Christ of Latter Day Saints, the group that built the polygamy compound, doesn't enter a goat racing team in the event.

The H&H Car Wash and Coffee Shop
El Paso

You can get your car washed by hand while you're sitting at the counter eating a carne picada burrito, an item so good that it was featured in *Saveur*, a cuisine magazine.

Ain't too many combination car wash/1950s-style dinettes that make it into fine-cooking publications. Come to think of it, ain't too many combination car wash/dinettes, period. But it must be working because this place, at 701 East Yandell Drive, has been in downtown El Paso since 1958.

"It was quite a unique idea my dad came up with, which has been, for the most part, real successful," said Kenneth Haddad, who owns H&H with his brother, Maynard.

★ ★

You get all sorts of characters coming into this place, which has a counter, three tables, and a bumper sticker on the ice machine that says STOP GLOBAL WHINING.

The Camino Real Hotel
El Paso

They ran a tight ship when they opened what was then called the Dream Hotel on Thanksgiving Day, 1912. According to literature put out by the hotel, house rules included:

1. "If you wet or burn your bed, you will be thrown out."
2. "You are not allowed downstairs in the seating room or in the kitchen when you are drunk."
3. "You must wear a shirt when you come into the seating room."

The lovely hotel is now the Camino Real and it's considerably looser, even offering dirty movies on its cable television system.

Before it became a hotel, the spot was the site of a saloon operated by Ben S. Sowell, who became the city's first mayor in 1873. As their first official act, Sowell and his aldermen made it illegal to bathe in the city's drinking water supply, an acequia that ran about 150 feet north of where the hotel is today.

El Paso was a rough-and-tumble town back then. A plaque on the hotel tells about how four men were shot dead in about five seconds at this location on April 14, 1881. But today, the hotel is still a jewel, featuring a Tiffany stained-glass dome, twenty-five feet in diameter, in the ceiling above the large, circular bar.

The Camino Real is just six blocks from Mexico. In the old days, hotel guests gathered at the rooftop ballroom and patio to watch the Mexican Revolution in progress across the Rio Grande. But the rooftop is no longer accessible to the public for liability reasons.

The hotel is located at 101 South El Paso Street. For more, call (905) 534-3000 or log on to caminoreal.com.

God Works in Mysterious Ways
Floydada

In August 1993, twenty people who had taken off from the small town of Floydada were found naked in the same car after it hit a tree in Vinton, Louisiana.

Darrell Gooch, a Floydada police officer at the time, said it all started when one of the group came home from the military. "He had a religious calling from God, telling him that the end of the earth was coming, and Floydada was where the initial disaster was going to start from," he said.

So why did they take off their clothes?

"The same one said the devil was in their clothing and all their possessions," Gooch recalled. "That's why they ended up as naked as jaybirds."

The former lawman said the car in which the people were stopped was "a little maroon Grand Am." News accounts said there were fifteen adults in the car and five children in the trunk. And no pants anywhere.

The incident brought a certain amount of fame to Floydada, although not necessarily the kind a Chamber of Commerce chairperson would relish.

"Even after all these years, we still get teased about being from Floydada," Gooch said.

The Lineaus Athletic Company
Fort Davis

"Right now, I make the best medicine ball in the world," said Lineaus Lorette. "I really do. I make a Cadillac . . . I make a Maserati . . . a Ferrari medicine ball."

Hardly anyone uses the big, clunky, heavy balls anymore. But Lineaus keeps making them anyway. He believes in them as a way to build upper body strength. He sells about thirty to forty a year.

**Lineaus Lorette claims to make the best
medicine balls in the world.**
JOHN KELSO

"As long as there's leather, I'll be making medicine balls," Lineaus
said. They're hand-sewn in a shop next to his house, surrounded by
the Davis Mountains. He used to make a twelve-sided ball but he's
upped it to a thirty-two-sided ball because it's a better ball.

"To make a round ball to last twenty years, you have to make small
panels," he explained. His standard model is fourteen inches in diameter, weighs usually ten to twelve pounds, and sells for $575. See them
at lineausathletic.com.

Paisano Pete, One Very Large Roadrunner
Fort Stockton

Ask former city tour guide Billy Twowalks Kail about the town's
eight-hundred-pound, twenty-foot-long roadrunner statue, known as
Paisano Pete, and you may learn more than you bargained for. This
guy knows his roadrunners.

★ ★

"He's a zygodoctile—he has two toes forward and two toes back," Kail said. "He's a member of the cuckoo family. He's one of two in the United States, the other being the rain crow. His main diet is rattlesnakes, baby quail, green lizards, and sparrows. He has an almost serpentine jaw. He swallows everything whole. He's very common to the entire Chihuahuan Desert. The word *paisano* means 'countryman.' And if you were in Italy, that would be 'friend.'"

Former Stockton police detective Sam Esparza's rendering of Paisano Pete.
SAMUEL R. ESPARZA

261

★ ★

There's more. His species name is *Geococcyx californianus*. He's called "the clown of the desert, and he doesn't fly well," Kail said. "He runs fast, flaps hard, and sails like a quail."

And you thought all roadrunners did was taunt Wile E. Coyote.

Once heralded by locals as the world's largest roadrunner, Paisano Pete has been dethroned by a monster bird outside of Las Cruces, New Mexico. But Pete appears content with being the world's second-largest from his post at the intersection of US Highway 290 and Main Street in downtown.

Really Big Cross
Groom

"I just wanted to advertise for our Creator in a bold manner," said Steve Thomas, a structural engineer from Pampa. "That's about as bold as you can get."

No kidding. The 190-foot-tall steel cross Thomas put up in 1995 on the south side of Interstate 40 at exit 212 is so big that you can see it up to twenty miles away. This cross, lit up at night, was billed as the largest cross in the Western Hemisphere until a 198-foot steel cross at Interstate 57 and Interstate 70 was completed in July 2001 in Effingham, Illinois.

"There's one other cross larger, and that's in Spain," Thomas said, speaking of a five-hundred-foot-tall masonry cross located sixty miles south of Madrid, built by Francisco Franco. Being a dictator, Franco probably didn't have to pay for it out of his own pocket. Thomas, however, spent five hundred thousand dollars of his own money to build this cross.

It's not just a cross, however. It is a cross complex with a big parking lot that will accommodate eighteen-wheelers, the Stations of the Cross done in bronze, and even a gift shop with indoor plumbing.

"We get one thousand or two thousand a day stopping, and ten million a year go by," said Thomas, who is head of an outfit called Cross of Our Lord Jesus Christ Ministries. He said he put up the cross to combat "X-rated stuff, period, not just on the highway," as well as alcohol and gambling.

In other words, the cross is lit up at night in hopes of keeping people from getting lit up at night.

You can't miss the second-largest cross in the Western Hemisphere. It's 190 feet tall.
JOHN KELSO

World's Largest Killer Bee
Hidalgo

The small town of Hidalgo on the Mexican border was the first in Texas to be visited by the deadly killer bees as they migrated north. So to take the sting out of the situation, the city commissioned and erected a giant killer bee—a nine-and-a-half- by ten- by twenty-one-foot statue to recognize the pests. It's big, it's yellow, and it sits in front of City Hall.

The killer bees reached Hidalgo on their march north in 1990.
JOHN KELSO

And the sculpture cost the city between sixteen and seventeen thousand dollars. That's a lot of honey.

The killer bees reached Hidalgo on October 15, 1990, according to the sign on the World's Largest Killer Bee.

There was some initial concern about what kind of negative effect it was going to have on the Rio Grande Valley, but rather than fret about it, the city decided to make lemonade out of lemons by putting up the statue. Now, thousands of tourists and curiosity-seekers come here every year to have their photos taken with the bee, and also spend some money, so a negative has been turned into a positive.

Hidalgo's giant bee has become famous, appearing in national magazines and newspapers, as well as the *Guinness Book of World Records*. And the Killer Bee ice hockey team represents the Rio Grande Valley in the Central Hockey League.

Stonehenge II
Ingram

It started out with one large stone. Doug Hill of Hunt was a tile contractor at the time, building a patio. When the job was completed, he had one stone left over. He asked his neighbor, Al Shepperd, if he wanted it. "He said, 'Let me put on my shoes. I'll show you where I want you to put it,'" Hill recalled. "We brought it over here and put it next to the road, and he said, 'I kinda like this rock.'"

The stone, about five feet, eight inches wide, was placed in a big field owned by Shepperd, across FM 1340 from Hunt's home. Once it was in place, Hunt noticed that Shepperd really admired the stone. "I'd see him driving by real slow, looking at his rock out there," Hunt said. "I thought it was a little odd, but he was a little eccentric anyway."

As time went by, Shepperd began mowing larger and larger circles around the stone. Then one day he showed up with an article about Stonehenge, the ancient Druid monument in England, and told Hunt, "I'd like you to build something behind that stone that looks something like this."

Doug Hill built this Easter Island figure and the Stonehenge re-creation nearby for his late neighbor, Al Shepperd. Shown with Hill are his three kids, Doug Jr. (with bike), Ella (the short one), and Sydney.

JOHN KELSO

★ ★

The end result is a ninety-two-foot-diameter hollow plaster re-creation of Stonehenge, flanked by two plaster Easter Island statues, one on each end of the field. Hunt said it took him and three laborers about four and a half months to build it. First, five arches of three fake stones each went up in the center. When that was done, Shepperd came into some money from the sale of a condominium so the crew started on the outside circle.

So why did Shepperd want this *objet d'art* on his land? "I think what inspired him was the publicity," Hunt said. When Shepperd passed away, his family scattered his ashes on the ground around Stonehenge II.

The family sold the land in 2010, and the Hill Country Arts Foundation in Ingram raised enough money to purchase the entire collection and move it to the foundation's property. The pieces were all numbered, dismantled, transported, and put back together so visitors can still view the unique attraction.

Deer Antler Tree
Junction

Don't lean up against this tree made of antlers, steel reinforcing rods, and chicken wire unless you want a hole poked in your jeans.

Texans tend to decorate with animal parts. So when members of the Kimble (County) Business and Professional Women's Club saw a fake tree made of deer antlers at the 1968 World's Fair in San Antonio, they figured they had to create their own version and display it in town.

The Junction model rises in front of Kimble Processing, a deer-processing plant, stands about fifteen feet high, and has hundreds of sets of antlers, some with skulls still attached. Most of the antlers are bleached out, so the look is somewhat parched. And don't expect any elk or moose antlers snuck in there. The locals maintain it's 100 percent deer.

A star sits atop the tree, and it gets lit up during the Christmas season. Since the tree has been around for more than forty years, it needs constant attention and add-ons because antlers tend to deteriorate, so the older ones are replaced when the need arises.

Sometimes uninformed persons from other states write to complain about people in Junction going out to shoot deer for the tree. But that's not true. Frederica Wyatt, curator the Kimble County Historical Museum, pointed out that some of the antlers were shed by the deer. "We don't just go out and shoot deer to get their antlers," she explained.

Chuck Eissler, the Toaster Guy
Kerrville

This thrice-retired dentist has more hobbies than Saturn has rings. Since Chuck Eissler is known as "the toaster man," you can probably guess one of them. He says it all began when his mother got a new pop-up toaster in the 1960s and he asked if he could have the 1926 Hotpoint "turner-flopper" that had resided on the kitchen countertop through his childhood.

Mom agreed. Later, his wife, Kay, brought home a similar one from a thrift store and sat it beside the old Hotpoint. The two looked pretty good together, so the collection started in earnest.

Now, nearly three decades later, his collection tops three hundred. The oldest is a 1912 General Electric model. Kay joined the fun as she researched, found, and framed the patent to hang beside the 1912 Pelouze.

"Toasters were patented in 1906," Eissler said. "You know, electricity was only for light bulbs at first. This [toaster] plugs into a light socket. There were no outlets back then."

His toaster collection lives in its own shelf-lined room, along with vintage toaster covers and toast racks. And he doesn't think present-day toasters have much character. "Early ones showed such ingenuity and creativity," he said while pointing out his "turner-floppers," "swingers," "side-loaders," "top-loaders," "flat beds," "pop-ups," "drop downs," and a "perco-toaster," which is a coffee percolator

Chuck Eissler, the Toaster Guy
AL BUCKNER

sitting atop a flat toaster. And the Mickey Mouse toaster not only imprints you-know-who on the toast, but also plays the catchy Mickey Mouse tune when it's finished.

Since no one disputes him, Eissler claims he has the largest toaster collection in Texas. And when he's not looking for more, he enjoys hanging out in his playhouse, strumming his guitar or reading about toaster collecting, which may be the best thing since sliced bread.

★ ★

The Graves Peeler Hall of Horns

Kingsville

It's really quiet in the separate room behind the John E. Conner Museum, where they store and display what Graves Peeler bagged while hunting. This is because all the animals in the room are dead.

It's a close, tight room with a low ceiling, and just about every square inch of wall space is covered with heads of critters, parts of

So where's the rest of the moose?
JOHN KELSO

critters, or whole critters. More than 250 of 'em, all mounted and glassy-eyed. There are full bears, bear rugs, a golden eagle, deer heads (some of them pairs of heads with their antlers tangled together), mountain goats, bighorn sheep, antelope, cow horns, javelina, and a half of a moose. The moose is taxidermied in such a way what when you look straight at it, it looks like a whole moose. But when you look from the side, you'll notice the back end is missing.

Graves Peeler was a Texas Ranger, cattle-brand inspector, rancher, and hunter. He shot his first white-tailed deer at the age of eight. That would have been in 1894. He lived until 1977, and he hunted all over North America. Local lore says that when Peeler's dad, a sheriff, was shot by three bad hombres, Peeler caught up with two of them and killed them in a gunfight. Later, the third one wrote Peeler from Louisiana, telling him he was ailing and wanted to return to Texas to die. Peeler allegedly wrote back that "you can come down here, but if you don't die, you know what's gonna happen—I'm gonna kill you myself." The man did return to Texas, so the story goes, but he died before Peeler could get to him.

Those who want to see the Peeler collection have to ask at the front desk of the museum, where someone on duty will grab the keys, unlock the door, and point the way in. The museum is located on the campus of Texas A&M University–Kingsville. For more information, call (361) 593-2810.

The Jersey Lilly Saloon
Langtry

From 1882 until his death in 1903, Judge Roy Bean served both justice and liquor out of the Jersey Lilly Saloon but, although the building still stands, don't get any ideas about finding a beer in this place. Located halfway between nowhere and too late to turn back, the bar was where Judge Bean handed out fines, sentences, and booze, either in the saloon or on the front steps because he was, at the time, "the law west of the Pecos."

These days the bare wooden building is run as a tourist attraction by the Texas Department of Transportation, and features a comfortable air-conditioned visitor center in the front section. You can learn quite a bit about Judge Bean at the alleged saloon by reading the historical marker and listening to the sound blurb that plays when you push the red button. When the transcontinental railroad came through this part of West Texas, the Texas Rangers needed someone to corral the drunks, so they made Judge Bean justice of the peace. The nearest courthouse was 125 miles away in Fort Stockton, so he basically fined the drunks and kept the money. He has been the subject of several movies and, despite what the films depict, he never sentenced anyone to death by hanging, or killed in any other fashion.

Incidentally, the saloon was named for English actress Lillie Langtry, whom Bean admired and for whom he named the town.

What's Your Major?
Levelland

Okay, kids, no fair looking at each other's work. Here are some of the questions on this semester's country-and-western music final:

1. True or False: George Jones was loaded when he hit that bridge.
2. Fill in the blanks: Let's go to Luckenbach, Texas, with _____, _____, and the _____.
3. What doesn't fit in this grouping: trains, mamma, gettin' drunk, pickup trucks, TGI Friday's?

Actually, those aren't real questions. But you really can get an associate of applied arts degree in country-and-western music from South Plains College in Levelland. (Since it's both country and western music, does that make it a double major?) Either way, South Plains College was the first of its kind in Texas to offer a degree plan specifically for country-and-western music.

After earning such a degree, the students are fully equipped to compete in the music business, whether it's as a performer, sound engineer, or camera operator. Or, perhaps, learning how to ride cross-country on a Greyhound bus.

The program has three recording studios—among them the Tom T. Hall Recording Studio and the Waylon Jennings Recording Studio. Students can also take private lessons on a variety of instruments, from mandolin to upright bass.

The school's alumni include Lee Ann Womack, Natalie Maines of the Dixie Chicks, Heath Wright of Ricochet, and Ricky Turpin, fiddle player with Asleep at the Wheel, among others.

Hand-Pulled Ferry
Los Ebanos

Want to cross the Rio Grande into Mexico in an unusual and old-fashioned way?

Then get yourself to Los Ebanos and ride the Los Ebanos Ferry.

It's the last hand-pulled ferry in the Western Hemisphere. A rope tethered on both banks runs from one side of the river to the other. A crew of four or five guys pulls the ferry across, hand-over-hand.

You can pitch a rock from Texas into Mexico at this location (or Mexico into Texas, depending on which side of the Rio Grande you happen to be standing on), so the trip takes only about four minutes.

Los Ebanos is two miles south of US Highway 83 on FM 886. The original ferry, which opened in 1950, could hold only two cars. But its newer replacement can transport three. It costs $2.50 to take a vehicle across the river, and that includes the driver. Additional passengers, or those who just walk on, are charged fifty cents each.

So who uses this unique ride? Mostly families visiting each other on both sides of the border. Snowbirds (people from up north who spend winters in Texas) are also regular customers. "I guess it's a novelty to see a ferry like this," a US Customs agent said.

But a word of caution: Be sure to take your passport along for the ride.

★ ★

Hey, will you lend a hand?
JOHN KELSO

The Stubbs Statue
Lubbock

Like most states, Texas is loaded with statues of generals, tycoons, and politicians. Finally, however, we get a statue of somebody who did something crucial for humanity: the barbecue man.

The seven-foot bronze statue of Christopher B. Stubblefield, whom everybody called Stubbs, stands at the site of his original barbecue joint at 108 East Broadway. The statue, by Santa Fe sculptor Terry

★ ★

Allen, shows Stubbs as he often appeared: in overalls and a cowboy hat, holding a plate of ribs.

Stubbs opened his barbecue joint in the late 1960s, and it soon became a favorite hangout for musicians. Joe Ely and Jesse Taylor started a Sunday-night jam session in the place. Artists such as Muddy Waters, Tom T. Hall, and Linda Ronstadt also would show up to play and eat.

Stubbs in bronze, with a plate of his world-famous ribs
JOHN KELSO

In the early 1990s, Stubbs appeared on David Letterman's show and fed barbecue to the audience. Stubbs had Letterman eating out of his hand, according to John Scott, who went into business with Stubbs in the 1990s and is one of the owners of Stubbs Barbecue in Austin.

Stubbs may be gone, but you can still see his face on his statue and on the bottles of his barbecue sauce, which is sold in an estimated thirty-five to forty thousand grocery stores around the world.

Shark Attack!
Marfa

Lunch trucks and "street food" may be popular in New York or San Francisco, but in Marfa, Texas? Most folks do a double take when they see the Food Shark parked under the pavilion between the railroad tracks and the Marfa Book Company.

The 1974 Ford van, a retired Butter Krust bread delivery truck, now has a kitchen and serving window where Krista Steinhauer whips up and serves up tasty cuisine she describes as "Mediterranean by way of West Texas." Open for lunch Tuesday through Friday and sometimes on Saturday, the Shark offers a menu of hummus, "Marfalafel," veggie wraps, Greek salad, and daily specials like shredded pork tacos, marinated chicken, roasted eggplant, or shrimp salad.

The Food Shark's outstanding fare has received rave reviews in dozens of magazines and newspapers, from *Bon Appetit* to the *New York Times*. But maybe the best part is that it's a fun gathering spot for locals, cowboys, and gallery-scene tourists.

For information, check out foodsharkmarfa.com or call (432) 386-6540.

Great food from the side of a truck
AL BUCKNER

The Mysterious Lights
Marfa

Who knows what causes those mysterious lights that come on and off in the distance? Whatever it is, the city makes hay out of it. About ten miles east of Marfa, on US Highway 90, you'll come to the mystery lights viewing area, a rest stop where you can pull over and look for the lights.

★ ★

The sign says MARFA MYSTERY LIGHTS VIEWING AREA. NIGHT TIME ONLY. Did they really need to put that notice on the sign? What kind of idiot would to look for lights in the sky during daylight?

John Kelso, author of *Texas Curiosities*, and a friend went to see the Marfa Lights on a Saturday night in July. "When we got there, the viewing area was packed," Kelso said. "Dogs were barking and people were yakking. A group of folks were looking at what they were pretty darned sure were the Marfa Lights. Just above the horizon, miles away, round white lights would come on, one at a time. Then they would burn out. Then they would come back on for a while. Then they would disappear again. They'd pop up in various spots."

There are several theories as to what causes the lights, which some say come in various colors and sometimes move around. Sightings have been recorded since 1883. Apaches believed they were stars falling to the earth. Others think they're probably a reflection of the stars below the horizon, bouncing off the atmosphere. Or maybe there's a guy off in the distance showing his vacation photos from Hawaii.

But whatever they are, Marfa plays them up. A banner on a local motel reads, SEE MYSTERY LIGHTS. On labor day, the city has a Marfa Lights celebration with a parade.

Tourists come from all over to see the lights. "Everybody's seen something different," said Pancho Borunda, who owns Borunda's Bar & Grill in Marfa. "In fact, we had some guys in here last night who had come all the way from Houston. They were asking questions like, 'When's the best time to see 'em, and should we bring some beer out there?'"

The answers to those two questions are (1) after dark, and (2) yes.

A Double Museum
McLean

This museum devoted to barbed wire is pretty sharp. And it's in the same building as the Route 66 Museum for a darned good reason. An average of between sixteen and eighteen thousand people go down Interstate 40 every day but not many of them stop when they see

★ ★

"Devil's Rope Museum." But when they see "Route 66 Museum," it's a different story. They slam on the brakes.

The building where these two museums co-exist used to be a brassiere factory called Marie Fashions. So visiting either one should be an uplifting experience. Under the circumstances, it also makes sense that the building houses a pair of museums.

The facility exists as a place for barbed wire collectors (there are about five hundred of them in the United States) to display their collections. There certainly are plenty of kinds of barbed wire to look at here. There are about 530 patented barbed wires, and the museum has collected about two thousand variations of those patents. They include barbed wire used by planters, barbed wire made for railroads, and barbed wire used in war—or, in other words, "war wire." In Texas, of course, this would be pronounced "war war."

The displays also include some plain old machine screw-ups, where the machine was worn or missed a lick somewhere along the line. Some people actually collect those things.

Also, there's barbed wire art, including *A Real Sharp Stetson*, a hat made entirely of barbed wire by an unnamed artist from Taos, New Mexico; a barbed wire jackrabbit; and a life-size barbed wire coyote.

The Route 66 Museum, put together by the Old Route 66 Association of Texas, starts out on a high note with a series of Burma Shave signs by the front entrance, including:

Don't stick your
Elbow out so far
It might go home
In another car.
Burma Shave

The museum's other highlights include an ancient restored Phillips 66 gasoline station, and the re-creation of the 66 Cafe that used to be located on the fabled road as it passed through McLean. The reproduction is vintage 1940s or 1950s, featuring a little four-stool counter,

May I take your order?
JOHN KELSO

dishes set out, and a lunch special board that tells you BLTs were forty cents. You want to know how dated this joint is? The place even has a cigarette machine.

Other artifacts include speakers from an old drive-in movie, a life-size doll of a sailor hitchhiking next to a Route 66 sign, and a key from Room 3 at the old Coral Courts Motel. The message "By the day or by the hour" is inscribed on the key. So, like the song says, people really did get their kicks on Route 66.

And as sort of a tribute to the brassiere factory once located here, hanging from the ceiling of the Route 66 Museum is an old road sign that says, 19 MILES TO MCLEAN, TEXAS, THE UPLIFT TOWN.

The dual museums are located at 100 Kingsley. You can trade barbs with the curators by visiting barbwiremuseum.com or calling (806) 779-2225.

National Cow-Calling Contest
Miami

Contestants in this national cow-calling event shoot for noise, not for style, so it gets pretty loud. Three judges are stationed about a half mile to a mile away from the platform where the contestants perform their cow calls. Whoever they can hear the loudest at that distance is named the winner. It's all about volume. Cows don't actually come running to town as a result of the callings.

The unique annual contest, held the first weekend in June, has been going on since 1949, and locals claim it's the only one of its kind in Texas, if not the entire United States.

The reason the contest is held here is that Roberts County (population about 550) is cattle country, so people are calling their cows anyway. They still get out of their pickups and call cows when it's feeding time, so they practice every day.

There are five divisions, one each for children, men, women, grandfathers, and grandmothers. Sometimes, each division will have as few as three entries, but other times there'll be as many as twenty. Those who want to enter should check out miamitexas.org.

Now That's a Lot of Concrete
Monahans

If you like to plan your vacation around places where you can look at enormous amounts of concrete, this is it.

The Million Barrel Museum is primarily an ill-fated ugly huge concrete tank built by Shell in 1928 to store oil. The company erected the semi-bowl-shaped monstrosity—the floor alone is large enough to hold five football fields—as a holding area for oil because at the time it didn't have enough pipelines to distribute the black gold.

A tent city grew up around the site during the construction. An army of men worked twenty-four hours a day on the project so it only took ninety days for completion. Maybe if they'd taken more time to build the tank, it wouldn't have started leaking oil so fast. But what

★ ★

Plan your next function here.
JOHN KELSO

really killed the endeavor was the stock market crash of 1929. The price of oil dropped from $1.75 a barrel to a nickel or a dime, so keeping oil around didn't seem quite so important.

So the tank sat there, gray and empty, until the 1950s, when an entrepreneur named Wayne Long bought it, primarily as a site for car races. But the concrete surface was so bumpy it tore the cars up, so that enterprise came to a sudden halt.

Then in 1958, the tank was used for a water park featuring a boat and ski show. But only for one day. Melody Park, named for Long's dog, opened and closed on October 5, 1958.

Over the years, it was put to other uses. In the early 1950s, promoters held square dances in the tank and drew up to 150 people on

★ ★

Friday nights. Later, some locals filled it with water and tried stocking it with trout. The trout died, apparently due to lack of vegetation and circulating water. In the 1970s, "some crazy local guys" tried to blow up the tank with a bomb, which explains some of the ruts in the floor.

These days the tank, which has an amphitheater on one end, is used for a variety of functions, including high school reunions and concerts. And the local high school kids scribble on the concrete walls—you know, stuff like "Natalie 'n' Gene."

There Are SOME Trees

Oh, yes, there are trees here in Notrees. Not many, but some. So that means this town of about twenty people is inappropriately named. Although just barely, because there aren't a lot of trees out here, about twenty miles west of Odessa. And the trees in Notrees are kind of droopy looking.

"There's a few elm, and some people have planted some pine trees now," said Jennifer Whitehead, postmaster of Notrees Post Office. Notrees also has an oil company and a volunteer fire department.

Whitehead said Charles Brown named the town in 1946, after moving here with his family. "He wanted to name the town Judy, for his third daughter," she said. "But when he sent the name to Austin, they wrote back that there was already a town named Judy. So he was looking out the window and noticed there were no trees. So he decided to name it Notrees."

★ ★

Oatmeal Festival
Oatmeal

There are several stories about how this small town (population twenty and located near Bertram) got its peculiar name. Some say it was because of a German named Habermill who settled the place in the 1840s. One version has it that "habermill" meant "oatmeal" in German, but German-speaking Germans say it doesn't.

Another version says the Scotch-Irish settlers who came after Habermill weren't able to pronounce the German's name correctly. And since "Habermill" sounded like "oatmeal" when they tried to say it the way Habermill did, it underwent the change.

Either way, each Labor Day there is an Oatmeal Festival. Oatmeal flakes are sprinkled out of small airplanes flying overhead, and there is an oatmeal bake-off. In the past, the festival also featured an oatmeal sculpture contest.

Ever thought about dropping cooked oatmeal out of a plane?

"Plop, plop, plop. I don't know about that," said Polly Krenek, Oatmeal's city secretary. "We'd have a lot of people [saying], 'Don't look up when the oatmeal plane's flying over. You'll get oatmeal in the face.'

"We still have some wacky games," Krenek added. "The oatmeal stacking and oatmeal-eating contest and that sort of thing."

Oatmeal stacking?

"You just take the regular oatmeal boxes, and whoever can stack the most and the highest wins," she explained.

It's easy to tell when you've reached Oatmeal. The town's water tower is painted red and gold to look like a Three-Minute Oats box.

Feeling a little flaky? Find out more about this anything-but-bland festival at oatmealfestival.com.

Guess what's for breakfast?
JOHN KELSO

★ ★

To Be or Not to Be
Odessa

This just doesn't seem like the sort of town where you'd find a re-creation of Shakespeare's Globe Theatre in London.

As you drive through Midland, Odessa's sister city next door out here in gas and oil country, you see a large sign next to the interstate that reminds you this was once the home of President George W. and Laura Bush. There aren't a lot of fuzzy-headed eggheads out this way, where oil is king. More common are bumper stickers with such messages as, IF MARY WAS PRO-CHOICE, THERE WOULD BE NO CHRISTMAS!

Still, Odessa College is the site of one of only three re-creations of Shakespeare's theater in the world.

There are some differences, of course. For one, Odessa's Globe has a roof on it. Also, there are seats in this one. In the original, there was a big open area where the lower classes, called "groundlings," would stand and watch the plays. So today's "groundlings"—the oil field roughnecks—can sit in comfort in this Globe in red plush upholstered chairs.

The idea for the theater popped up when the late Marjorie Morris, a high school English teacher, gave her students an assignment to build models of Shakespeare's Globe. When one of her students commented that it would be "neat" to have such a facility in Odessa, the idea was planted. Work began shortly afterward, and the theater opened in 1968.

This Globe also comes with a re-creation of Anne Hathaway's cottage next door. But it doesn't have a thatched roof for a couple of reasons. For one, the fire marshal wouldn't allow it because of the fire hazard it would create in this dry desert climate. One little spark would spell doom for the structure, just like one little spark from a cannon burned down the Globe in London around 1613. Also, there's not much thatch available in West Texas and importing the stuff would have come at an astronomical cost.

Ann Wilson in the Globe Theatre—that's "thee-A-ter" to you
JOHN KELSO

On the other hand, just like in Shakespeare's Globe, this theater has three Old English–style turrets above the stage known as "the heavens." In Shakespeare's day, characters coming out of "the heavens" were lowered down to the stage by cable. But they don't do that in Odessa because it's too dangerous.

People come from hundreds of miles away to attend the plays. Among them was a reporter from London, sent here to do a story on the Texas Globe. He was probably very impressed when he learned that once a month, this Globe features a show of country or gospel music, or a combination of the two. Hamlet and Haggard: no place but Texas.

For more information, punch up globesw.org or call (432) 332-1586.

It's a Bird, It's a Plane, It's a Really Large Hunk of Iron
Odessa

The West Texas desert is a great place for a meteor to land because it ain't going to get much uglier even after something big hits it. Except for the pump jacks and scrub brush, there isn't much to look at in the oil patch.

Of course, there was even less going on sixty-three thousand years ago when a 250-ton chunk of mostly iron slammed into the ground at seven miles a second. That's twenty-five thousand miles an hour.

The Odessa Meteor Crater, about five hundred feet in diameter, was about one hundred feet deep at the time of impact. But at its current depth of about twelve feet, this crater, the second largest of its kind in the United States, isn't nearly as impressive as it was in its youth. After the explosion, about fifteen feet of rubble that had blown up in the air fell back into the depression. Then the sand started blowing and almost filled it up. Now the crater is shallow enough that you can take a walking tour through it without worrying about busting your butt. On the other hand, there's a sign at the beginning of the tour that tells you to watch out for snakes.

There's also a museum on the site, and you can go through the whole thing (maybe we should say "the hole thing") in an hour. You can see various chunks of the actual Odessa meteorite, although they aren't exactly sexy in color, since the space visitor was 90 percent iron. They're brown on the outside due to rusting, which means they don't clash with the area's ubiquitous oil field equipment. But if you cut into one, they're shiny and metallic on the inside.

They're also heavy. In the mid-1970s, somebody stole the largest specimen—a 105-pound hunk—from an earlier museum. And the thieves wouldn't have needed a truck to do it because a 105-pound meteorite sample is no bigger than a basketball.

The site and museum are located on Interstate 20, exit 108. For more information, call (432) 381-0946.

This meteorite weighs seventy pounds, but others in
the museum are no bigger than a grain of sand.
JOHN KELSO

World's Largest Jackrabbit

Odessa

The best part about this big-eared, eight-foot-tall fiberglass statue is
the jackrabbit recipe on the back of one of the two plaques next to it.
It says: "First, catch your rabbit. Dress rabbit. Salt and soak in brine,
then boil 'til tender. Add pepper to taste. Fill pot with dumplings.
Cook 'til dough is done."

Seeing the world's largest jackrabbit in Odessa is a hare-raising experience.
JOHN KELSO

Recipes like that explain why Kentucky Fried Chicken was invented.

One marker tells about how jackrabbits can do forty-five miles an hour, and that they were a "prized" source of food among the Indians. Hey, if you were a prized food among the Indians, you'd do forty-five miles per hour, too.

The other marker addresses the alleged 1932 Odessa Rodeo's First Championship Rabbit Roping. The alleged event allegedly was won by Grace Hendricks, who allegedly beat out several male competitors by allegedly roping a jackrabbit from horseback in five seconds flat. There are no videos of the alleged event.

Incidentally, the World's Largest Jackrabbit, as it has been billed, now has offspring: Thirty-six additional jackrabbits sprang up all over town in April 2004 through February 2005. It was called the Jackrabbit Jamboree. The Odessa Convention and Visitors Bureau solicited artists in the Permian Basin area to submit their concept of what they would do to alter a rabbit's appearance, then held a juried show where people selected the ones they wanted to be put on display.

Among those commissioned were *Jacks Are Wild* (a rabbit covered with playing cards), *Hare on a Hog* (a rabbit in biker attire), and *Gusher the Hare* (a rabbit sporting a drawing of an oil well).

The new rabbits were spread all over town, but the big one still sits on the corner of Eighth Street and North Sam Houston Avenue.

Dan Blocker Bust
O'Donnell

The bronze bust of Dan Blocker, the big guy who played Hoss Cartwright on the TV western *Bonanza*, can be found on a pedestal right across the street from the museum that has the Dan Blocker Room. Of course, nearly everything is right across the street in O'Donnell since there are only about one thousand people living here. Blocker grew up here, and his parents ran the Blocker Grocery. That explains the bronze bust, done by noted sculptor Glenna Goodacre, who also did the Vietnam Women's Memorial.

The Blocker bust reads: THANKS TO FILM, HOSS CARTWRIGHT WILL LIVE. But all too seldom does the world get to keep a Dan Blocker.
ELAINE PEARSON

The O'Donnell Heritage Museum has a pair of Blocker's boxing mitts, a *Bonanza* lunch box, a photo of Blocker's fourth-grade class, and other Hoss Cartwright memorabilia, including the Boy Scout pants he wore when he was probably eleven or twelve years old. They're big. Really big. Big for an eleven- or twelve-year-old, probably big for a forty-year-old. In fact, Blocker's Scout britches may be big enough to house a Cub Scout pack.

★ ★

Musical Welding Job
Pampa

Walter Russell "Rusty" Neef's 150-foot-long steel score of the chorus to Woody Guthrie's "This Land Is Your Land" is so accurate that
a musician could read it like a piece of sheet music. And without as
much eye strain. The treble clefs are twelve feet high.

"It is musically correct," said Neef, a welder since 1946 who spent
about four hundred hours in 1993 creating the work, now located in
front of the M.K. Brown Civic Center on Hobart Street. "You could
play it or sing it or whatever, if you knew what you were looking at."

If you can read music, you can play "Rusty" Neef's steel score to
the chorus of Woody Guthrie's "This Land Is Your Land."

Neef admits he wouldn't know what he was looking at. "I know nothing whatsoever about music," he said. "That puts me in a very awkward place." So he had Wanetta Hill, a music teacher in the Pampa school system, arrange the score for him in the key of G and 4/4 time.

The Guthrie song was picked for the project because the folksinger lived in Pampa in the late 1930s and early 1940s. Neef didn't know him, but remembers seeing him on the streets. "In fact, they like to brag this is where he started writing his music," Neef said. "I don't think that's correct, but it makes a good story."

Neef is proud of his project, which he said should last for eighty to one hundred years because nothing but the best materials were used. For example, the paint cost $125 a gallon. Neef spent a little over eighteen thousand of his own money to build the Gurthrie chorus, and then presented it to the city. He said he made the work to leave something behind to honor his father, George Herman Neef, who started the family's welding shop here in 1936.

And the work is colorful, no doubt about it. "I thought it was so attractive that I lighted it with red, white, and blue lights," Neef said. "It is a patriotic song, so the first section is red, the second one is white, and the third one is blue."

Some Really Big Goobers
Pearsall and Floresville

Ironically, the World's Largest Peanut, which really isn't all that large, sits in front of Randall Preston Produce, a potato business, on Oak Street in Pearsall. And lots of folks come through Pearsall just to see the giant goober.

But, although it claims to have the globe's giantest goober, the town holds a Potato Festival instead of a Peanut Festival. However, the reason the big peanut is in Pearsall is that Pearsall is in a peanut-growing area and boasts about it through the slogan on the peanut statue's concrete base. It reads: PEARSALL, TEXAS—WORLD'S LARGEST PEANUT—55,000,000 LBS. MARKETED ANNUALLY.

In Floresville they're nuts over peanuts.
JOHN KELSO

★ ★

Floresville also has a big peanut, prominently displayed on the Wilson County Courthouse lawn with its own spotlight.

Designed by builder Richard Ullmann, the concrete nut harkens back to a day when many peanuts were grown around these parts. And while Pearsall has the largest peanut but no Peanut Festival, Floresville settles for one big nut—and a Peanut Festival. It's been going on since 1944 and lasts for an entire week every October. They crown a peanut king and queen; the queen gets the exotic name of Queen Tunaep, and her male counterpart is called King Reboog. (He also gets to appear at public functions wearing a cowboy hat covered with unshelled peanuts.)

Sheets to Oil Wells
Post

It is not true that every house in Texas has an oil well in the yard. On the other hand, Post is the kind of town where people are glad to see the price of gasoline go up. Oil wells are so prevalent that you can sometimes see them operating on the Garza County Courthouse lawn. At one time, in 2006, there were sixty-eight producing wells in this city of about four thousand situated at the intersection of US Highway 84 and US Highway 380.

Ah, but it was not always this way. In the past, instead of oil, it was bed sheets and pillowcases. The town was founded in 1907 by eccentric wealthy man C. W. Post, the creator of Post Cereals. He started the town with the utopian idea of building a model self-contained community.

Post began operations out here when it was buffalo and Indian country. He started by buying about 333 square miles of prairie land. Then he had small farmhouses built and sold them to settlers who wanted to grow cotton.

Post spent $650,000 to build the enormous 444,000-square-foot Postex Cotton Mills, a bed-sheet and pillowcase manufacturing plant that had its own cotton gin, boiler operation, and weaving room. The plant was completed in 1911. The farmers living in the little farmhouses would grow the cotton and provide it to Postex, where plant employees would make the sheets.

It was the first operation to grow the cotton, process it, convert it into product, and market it, all in the same facility. The plant, later taken over by Burlington Industries, operated until 1983. During that time, former employees remember, a tongue twister was posted on the plant walls. It read:

I slit a sheet, a sheet I slit,
Upon a slitted sheet I sit.
I'm not a sheet slitter, or a sheet slitter's son,
But I'll slit sheets 'til the sheet slitter comes.

Say that three times without screwing up, and you might get yourself a radio job.

Post's stamp can still be found all over town. The beautiful redbrick streets are his work. His statue stands in front of the courthouse. And the local paper is called (what else?) the *Post Dispatch*.

Incidentally, Old Mill Trade Days, with 100 to 140 vendors, still take place at the old Postex plant Friday through Sunday the first weekend of each month. So if you're lucky, you might be able to find one of the old bed sheets made at the plant. But there aren't any tongue-twister signs left.

Presidential Treatment
Stonewall

President Lyndon Baines Johnson had a wicked sense of humor. When people would visit his ranch in Stonewall, outside Johnson City, he loved to take them for a ride in his little blue '62 model Amphicar built in West Germany. Of course, he didn't tell them that the vehicle was amphibious.

★ ★

As he hollered that the brakes had failed, he'd run the vehicle into the Pedernales River as a joke. The convertible is still on display in the carport at the ranch.

Running his funny little car into the water wasn't President Johnson's only quirk. The late George Christian, LBJ's press secretary from 1966 to 1969, said the president was a gregarious fellow who didn't like being alone but he never quit working. So he'd keep talking to his staff "while he was shaving, while he was showering, while he was on the pot, or whatever," Christian said. "He just kept on going. . . . It didn't bother me seeing him naked, which was often, or in his pajamas."

Christian recalled the time the president accidentally drenched him with his Water Pik. "One time, he was brushing his teeth and I was standing in the doorway taking notes, and Larry Temple [the president's attorney] was standing right behind me," he said. "And he [LBJ] looked up at me while he was using that Water Pik and squirted me from head to toe with Lavoris. The president just kept going. And I spent the rest of the day smelling like mouthwash."

Another thing Johnson would do was eat your food as a joke. "When he was on a diet, which was all the time, he'd reach over and steal your ice cream," Christian said. "He didn't ask you, he just did it. He'd sit there and stare at your dessert, and the next thing you know, here comes this big old hand stealing your dessert or your butter."

It's a Jungle Out There
Tarzan

How did Tarzan, a ranching and farming community in a flat place, get its name?

According to information available at the little Tarzan post office, the town was founded in 1924 by Tant Lindsay, who later submitted a list of six names for the community. All six were rejected by the Post Office Department in Washington, DC, because they were already being used in Texas. Lindsay submitted four more lists; every name on them was also turned down for the same reason.

So for the sixth list, Lindsay sent in six names from the Edgar Rice Burroughs book, *Tarzan, Lord of the Jungle*, which he had just bought for his daughter. The names were Lord, Jungle, Edgar, Rice, Burroughs—and Tarzan.

Washington approved Tarzan.

Scandal Rocks Chili Cook-off

Terlingua

Don Eastep had no idea he'd win the thirty-seventh annual Original Terlingua Frank X. Tolbert-Wick Fowler Chili Cook-off when he turned in a bunch of chili samples he didn't even cook.

"How could you possibly win with a conglomeration of chilis?" a sheepish Eastep said in 2003, after he'd been busted for cheating at this cook-off in the desert, considered the grand-daddy of them all. "That was the last thought in my mind—that it would win. And when it did, there was nobody who was more shocked."

Eastep, who wasn't even qualified to enter the cook-off, said it all started out as a joke. Posing as his brother, Larry Eastep, who had qualified to cook but didn't attend, Don Eastep took a tasting cup around to the various cooks and got them to toss dollops of their chili into his cup.

Then Don transferred the mix into his brother's entry cup, entered the chili—and won. When he was announced as the winner from the podium, he said he was "absolutely stunned." Then when the officials found out what had happened, Eastep had to give back the trophy and other awards.

"The bottom line is, I should not have done it," he said later. "And when they called the winning number, I wish at this instant that I would not have responded."

Tom Noll, one of the judges fooled by the phony entry, later joked, "We caught the scoundrel, the Benedict Arnold that he is. We've got to set up guards at the border to make sure he never comes back."

★ ★

The Tolbert-Fowler event is one of two big chili cook-offs held in Terlingua on the first Saturday in November. The other one, the Chili Appreciation Society International Cookoff, had nothing to do with the 2003 scandal.

For more information, log on to abowlofred.com or call (817) 421-4888 for the Tolbert-Fowler contest; and chili.org or (888) 227-4468 for the other.

Prada of West Texas
Valentine

Out in this section of far West Texas, folks march to distinctly different drummers, and nobody cares. Maybe those "Marfa mystery lights" have something to do with it. Anyway, Prada Marfa is defined by its creators as "a pop architectural land art project." Most folks, however, define the single-story structure as "What the hell is that?"

It sits all by itself out in the middle of nowhere, about a mile and a half northwest of Valentine, which is about thirty-two miles northwest of Marfa on US Highway 90. The sculptors, Michael Elmgreen, a Dane, and Ingar Dragset, a Norwegian, who now live in Germany, are acclaimed for their works of wit, whimsy, and sometimes subversive looks at the cultural world around them. Many think Prada Marfa is a surrealist commentary on Western materialism.

Miuccia Prada herself was consulted, personally chose the pseudo-store's merchandise, and gave permission to use the Prada logo. Built at a cost of eighty thousand dollars and opened October 1, 2005, it's made of biodegradable adobe that will slowly melt back into the landscape. Although designed never to need repairs, the artists apparently never heard of vandals. Within three days after the opening, all the handbags and shoes were stolen and the walls decorated with graffiti.

Repaired and restocked, the new store is a booby trap for thieves. The walls and windows are strong, the shoes fit the right feet only, and the purses have no bottoms, hiding part of the security system. In

Only one question: Why?
AL BUCKNER

a place known for its bizarreness, this may be one of the most bizarre. And thousands of visitors each year stop at the fake store in the middle of nowhere.

The John Madden Haul of Fame
Van Horn

There isn't much to do in Van Horn, and the John Madden Haul of Fame doesn't much correct the situation.

Located at 1200 West Broadway, in the John Madden Room of Chuy's Restaurant, the shrine to ex-coach/commentator/TV pitchman has pictures of retired football players Mike Singletary and Anthony Muñoz and the chair Madden sits in when he visits the place to eat chicken picado, his favorite. The chair has Madden's name on the back, like a director's chair. And the table—right in front of the big television screen—has a sign on it that tells you it is RESERVED FOR JOHN MADDEN.

Chuy's owner, Chuy Uranga, said the former NFL TV commentator stops in two or three times a year during coast-to-coast trips in his

Sweethearts Day

Thanks to the name Valentine, this place is transformed into a veritable Cupid City in mid-February each year.

Around Valentine's Day, the two-woman post office in this town of fewer than two hundred residents gets nearly twenty thousand Valentine cards from hither and yon, each one looking to be stamped with an illustration done by Valentine eighth-grader Veronica Calderon. Her design showed a cowboy on a horse throwing a rope in the shape of a heart, with the words "Love Station" inside the loop. It was created in 2003 to mark the twentieth anniversary of the Valentine post office's Valentine's Day stamp program.

So what you have is two gals stamping thousands of Valentines, one right after the other—clonk, clonk, clonk, etc. Doesn't that get to be a pain in the behind? "It gets a little hectic, but we enjoy it," said Maria Carrasco, the postmaster. "We get our workout for the year." They probably also get repetitive stress syndrome.

This Texas Valentine is one of only three towns with that name in the United States. The others are Valentine, Nebraska, and Valentine, Arizona. There's also a Valentines in Virginia. As far as anyone knows, however, there is no town named Custody Battle, Montana.

★ ★

tour bus. Madden hates flying, so he travels cross-country from one broadcasting job to the next in his own bus.

The shrine is called the "Haul" of Fame because Madden told Uranga that having it in the restaurant "would haul people here." And Uranga says it has.

Madden really is a big Chuy's fan. He even mentions the place in glowing terms in his book, *John Madden's Ultimate Tailgating*, by commenting:

"If I stop at my favorite Mexican restaurant (Chuy's in Van Horn, Texas, a contributor to the recipe section of this book), I will take the chicken and rice and the beans and mix them all up because that was what I did as a kid." The book includes Chuy's recipes for tamales, steak picado, and Spanish rice and beans.

Madden has been stopping at Chuy's on his way across America since 1987, Uranga said. The story goes that on one of his trips, he was looking for a place that had his two favorite things: football on TV and Mexican food. Chuy's had both.

To check it out, call (432) 283-2066 or see chuys1959.com.

The Roy Orbison Museum
Wink

If you wink going through Wink, you'll miss the Roy Orbison Museum on TX 115. And that would be a shame, because you wouldn't get to try on the late singer's famous prescription sunglasses.

Roy Orbison, he of "Oh, Pretty Woman" fame, may have had a uniquely haunting voice, but his eyes apparently weren't much. If you have average eyes, when you look through his prescription sunglasses, it's kind of like opening your eyes underwater.

The sunglasses were donated to the museum by Barbara Orbison, Roy's widow. If you do try them on, curator Dorothy Wolf will take a Polaroid picture of you wearing them, if you wish. Then she'll ask you to autograph it, and she'll tack it to the wall. So the one-room museum has a bunch of goofy-looking photos of people wearing Roy Orbison's sunglasses.

Roy Orbison planned "to lead a Western Band" and "marry a beautiful dish."
JOHN KELSO

Orbison grew up in Wink and graduated from high school here in 1954. Wolf, who knew him back then, said he was "a humble sort of fella. He was pretty shy, pretty introverted, except for his music. There isn't any scandal about him. The boys would go somewhere, and he'd be the designated driver. And he couldn't see. He was really blind. So they weren't much better off."

At the museum, you can see all manner of Orbison memorabilia, including records, photos, high school yearbooks, and a poster from *The Fastest Guitar Alive*, a 1968 movie in which he starred. It was not well-received. In his 1998 *Movie & Video Guide*, film critic Leonard Maltin noted: "Doomed effort to turn recording star Orbison into a movie star—with the dumbest title imaginable for a Civil War espionage story!"

A recent addition to the museum's collection is a traffic sign that warns: TOW AWAY ZONE—ORBISON FANS PARKING ONLY.

Each year, the museum holds a Roy Orbison Festival on the weekend closest to April 23, his birthday. Want to guess what they call the festival's beauty pageant? The Pretty Woman Pageant. What else could they possibly call it?

If you're interested in seeing the museum, call Wink City Hall at (432) 527-3441. It's by appointment only.

The Wink Sinks
Near Wink

Used to be that there was only one Wink Sink, a big hole in the ground off CR 205 that appeared mysteriously almost overnight in the oil fields between Kermit and Wink in 1980. But now there are two Wink Sinks—thanks to a second large hole discovered in the ground in May of 2002 about a half mile southeast of the original Wink Sink.

This is a good part of the world for large holes to appear, since it's so flat, making them easy to find. Besides, not many people live out this way, so it's less likely for somebody to be standing over a large hole when it decides to show up.

Not that you could miss these holes. The first Wink Sink is no slouch in the size department—probably a hundred yards wide, according to local officials. But it's no match for the new crater, which is even more humongous.

The newcomer is quite a bit larger and deeper than the other, officials said. It's probably 200 yards by 150 yards wide and 188 feet down to the water from the surface of the ground. Right now, nobody knows for sure how deep the water is.

You can drive right up to the old one and get a good look at it, but the newer one is harder to reach. There's a fence around it with a locked gate and signs that say DANGEROUS and KEEP OUT. And, officials warn, it's best not to go in there because the ground is still very unstable.

So why are large holes popping up unannounced in this part of the world? According to an area geologist, there's a fault that runs from

Carlsbad Caverns to Sonora Caverns, and these two sinkholes are on that fault, and it continues to grow. The geologist said this was the most active phenomenon of its type in the nation.

So next time you blink, there might be a third Wink Sink.

Frigid Fight Song
Winters

In many places in Texas, it's a cold day if the dog's water bowl freezes an eighth of an inch on the back porch. Chili we know better than chilly, if you catch the drift.

But because of the town name, in Winters they play the cold theme up big. The high school band uses the mellow "Walkin' in a Winter Wonderland" as the school's fight song. A song popularized by Guy Lombardo and his Royal Canadians ends up as a Texas fight song? Go figure.

Actually, the fight part of the song is buried in the middle of the tune. The song starts out "bump bah bah, dah dah dah dah," real upbeat, but about halfway through it goes into an actual fight song. And for whom are they fighting?

The Blizzards, of course.

Because Winters High School is the home of the Fightin' Blizzards.

Even though you wouldn't think people would get real fired up with a song that starts out, "Sleighbells ring, are you listenin'?" the song has been used for quite some time at football games here.

Winters High also uses other wintery themes. Back in the 1960s, they had a little jazz combo called the Snowmen, and they have the Glacier King and Queen event every year. What they don't have is a ski area. And most of the ice comes in a plastic bag. Despite the name, this ain't Colorado.

In reality, the town name has nothing to do with the climate. According to *The New Handbook of Texas*, Winters was named for John N. Winters, a rancher and land agent who donated land for the first school.

index

index

index

index

index

index

about the author

★ ★

Sam Lowe has been living in and writing about the Southwest since 1969. He worked as a columnist for the *Phoenix Gazette* and *Arizona Republic* for more than twenty-five years and was once named "Humor Columnist of the Year" by the National Society of Newspaper Columnists.

He entered a state of semiretirement in 1999 to become a freelance writer. His work has appeared in such publications as *Arizona Highways*, *Arizona Highroads*, *Sedona Magazine*, *Scottsdale Scene*, and *International Travel and Tourism News* and several newspapers, including the *Arizona Republic*, *USA Today*, *Chicago Tribune*, and *Columbus Dispatch*. He is also the author of *You Know You're in Arizona*, *Arizona Curiosities*, and *New Mexico Curiosities*, for Globe Pequot Press.

Lowe, his wife, Lyn, and their dog, Zach, live in Phoenix.